ACKNOWLEDGMENTS

When I first thought about writing a book I had no idea of the number of people who have affected my life and therefore helped me to get to this point. My first thanks must go out to my Mom and Dad, who taught me to be independent and to work hard. I wish they were around to enjoy this with me.

To my fraternity brothers at the Oregon State University Sigma Chi house, especially Dave Peoples, Steve Miller, Peter Potwin and Mark Stewart; any time I asked any of them for help they have always given it to me NO questions asked.

Frank Ramsey had the faith in me to help me start my first business; without that I have no idea where I would be. Bob Collins for joining me when I first started Huntington Property Services and buying it when I left.

Larry Pothast, Mike Kennedy, and Katherine Young, those crazy bankers who first showed me there was a future in banking community associations. Had Bob Skertich not introduced me to Ray Lamb I have no doubt my life would be much different. It was one of the saddest days of my life when Bob's wife Bonnie told me Bob passed away. He was one of the kindest men I have ever met.

Bob and Sue Stewart, my surrogate parents. After my father died 20 years ago, they were always there when I needed a father's advice.

My wife Deborah and my two boys, Craig Lee and Matt, have given me the reason to continue to fight even when it seemed I had no fight left. Especially my son Craig Lee, who had many great opportunities when he graduated from Georgetown but decided to help his old man when we had to start all over. It was Craig Lee who worked 80 to 100 hours a week on all the details necessary to start a new banking division. He is also responsible for most of my PowerPoint presentations.

God gave me the gift of gab so I have always used that to make my point. Putting my thoughts on paper would never have been possible without the help and support of Mark Graham. His ability to take my thoughts and put them on paper is remarkable.

Then, of course, there is Ray Lamb. Ray gave me the break of a lifetime. His confidence and support allowed me to build the largest HOA specialty banking program in the country.

Finally, thank you to Robert Sarver, CEO of Western Alliance Bancorp. Robert has stuck with me through some very rough times. My next book will detail the growth of AAFS to the top of the Association Banking world.

TABLE OF CONTENTS

FOREWORD

Throughout this book I discuss how taking risks can help you achieve your dreams and goals. I think it important to talk about what motivates us to take these risks. In my life, there have always been four indisputable passions:

Family
God
Country
Job

From the day I hired my first employee at the F.U.B.A.R. in 1973, I always made sure anyone who worked for me was aware of my philosophy: *Family Always Comes First.* Too many times we get so involved in our business ventures we forget why we are doing what we are doing. Having goals and dreams is very important, but they should never be at the expense of your family.

I was very lucky as I grew up in a very intact family. For the most part, my mother stayed home and took care of her four children and my father worked to support us. True, there were times growing up that I resented the fact that Dad was a workaholic. He made it to very few of my Little League games or school programs. As I grew older, I discovered that he was doing what he thought was right, and I admired him for this. Growing up during the Depression, Dad had very little. He was determined that his family would want for nothing and, most important, that all his children were able to attend college, an opportunity he never had. As it turned out, all four of Dad's children graduated from college and, because of his tireless work, did so without the burden of student loans.

My father taught me what you could achieve if you worked hard and never gave up. This was an extraordinary gift.

As for Mom, I cannot remember her ever saying a bad word about a single person. She taught me that it takes all types of people and personalities to make this world go around and that we should respect everyone. Most of all, Mom taught me independence. I can remember growing up on Mercer Island in the 60s and asking her for a ride somewhere. "You have two feet and a thumb," she would reply. Unlike many parents today, Mom did not make us live in a bubble. She wanted us to go out and experience life, and this turned out to be the best gift a parent could give a child.

My wife Deborah and I have also tried to raise our children to be independent. Fortunately, with the changes in technology, I was able to work as hard as my father did, while still managing to be at home for many of the special moments in my kids' lives. Because of the business I had chosen, being home for dinner every night was not always possible, so we had breakfast every morning as a family. I believe this all-important family time helped my two boys become the successful men they are today.

Always make time for your family: you can do no better than that. When you leave this world, they will be the ones who remember your actions more than anyone. Make those actions memorable.

Chapter 1

Leadership is a Verb

Taking Action

If you take only one thing from this book, it will be a new definition for the word: Leadership.

Forget what you learned in fifth grade English. Forget what you read in Webster's Collegiate Dictionary.

Leadership is not a noun. Sure, you've heard it defined as "the function of a leader" or "the act of giving guidance or direction." All well and good, except it misses the point.

Leadership is not an adjective. It is not a word that describes a man or a woman with a title after his or her name, though we would all love that to be true. Do you have any idea how many CEOs, department heads, and business owners there are who don't have a clue about what true leadership is? About what it takes to define a strategy and give people the motivation to bring that strategy to life? The short answer: a lot.

No, leadership is not a noun or an adjective.

**Leadership is a verb. It is defined very simply to mean:
taking action.**

A true leader – someone who takes action not only in business, but also in his or her personal life, in the community, and in the world – makes things happen. A true practitioner of leadership leads by example, by doing, by getting his or her hands dirty. A true practitioner of leadership is a person who is willing to make mistakes and profit by those mistakes, a person who is willing to jump into the fray and come out of it a little bloodied if necessary. That's leadership.

Take-action leadership not only shows people where you and your company are headed or what your goals in life may be, but it also motivates them to jump into the fray with you and get things done.

Take-action leadership defines your purpose – the Japanese call it *mokuhyou* (attaining your purpose) and the Chinese call it *yiyi* (sense of purpose). In other words, a man or woman who acts on his or her purpose, as opposed to sending it out in a memo or an email, brings it to life. You're showing them, not just telling them. You're sharing a roadmap, as it were, because people can actually see the road you're traveling down.

Make leadership a verb. Take action.

———

When you do, you'll not only become a great leader and a great inspiration for those around you, you'll also provide the kind of direction that will make the world a better place.

———

And what could be better than that!

Thinking Different

I grew up on Mercer Island in the great state of Washington, just across the bridge from Seattle.

I graduated from Mercer Island High School so long ago that Lewis and Clark were just getting their first glimpse of the Pacific Ocean. Well, maybe not quite that long ago, but it was during this time of my life that I first discovered a tool that would last me my entire life: *Thinking Different.*

I mention this because Mercer Island, a town populated with doctors, lawyers, and Indians Chiefs, is not only a fine and secure place to grow up, it is the kind of place where a rigid set of expectations flourishes. You're raised with not-so-subtle hints about becoming a doctor, lawyer, or Indian Chief. There was never a question about any of us going to college – that was a given – the only question was where.

For the vast majority of my fellow graduates, the answer to this question of where they would eventually hang their collegiate hat came from a very familiar, very predictable list: the University of Washington, Washington State, Central Washington, or maybe Western Washington. You see the trend here. Take your choice. We had a guy at our high school named Steve Hawes. Steve could play basketball like nobody's business. He received scholarship offers from all across the country. But Steve had been programmed like all the rest of us and chose University of Washington. I'm not criticizing – the U of W is a fine school – I'm just illustrating the trend.

What makes this even more interesting is that this was 1968, the era of free love and freethinking. Weren't we supposed to be "questioning authority"? Weren't we supposed to be "doing our own thing"? Not if you grew up on Mercer Island. We had all lived sheltered, privileged lives, so why rock the boat?

Not me. I was a born boat-rocker. I liked making waves, because it made life more interesting. Now don't get me wrong; I was not a troublemaker. I don't want to imply that. Actually, I've always been a flag-waving, law-abiding redneck kind of guy, to tell you the truth. But that, I discovered early on, has nothing to do with "thinking differently." So maybe I'm talking about "internal" rocking the boat; in other words, making waves in the way we approach our daily lives.

Thinking different isn't a matter of politics or religion, social standing or buying power. Thinking different is a state of mind that looks for challenges and opportunities and isn't afraid of a little risk.

I admit it: I did go through the motions of applying to the University of Washington, not 20 minutes from my home, and I was probably somewhat relieved when I was accepted. But I had also applied to a half dozen other schools in Oregon and California, and when I opened my acceptance letter from Oregon State inviting me to spread my educational wings in a place called Corvallis, Oregon, I knew this was an opportunity I couldn't pass up. Here was a chance to act on my instinct to think differently, to take a risk, and move outside my comfort zone.

The Courage to Act

Maybe "courage" isn't the right word. Maybe it's having the guts to act. Maybe it's having the audacity to say, "What's the worst that can happen?"

All I know is that sometimes you have to put yourself in situations that aren't particularly comfortable and that don't feel all that safe and secure, situations where your only alternative is to act. And not just to make do, and not just to get by. I'm talking about jumping in feet first, determined to make the most of the situation and even to turn it to your advantage. That is what living is all about.

André Malraux, the French adventurer and statesman, once wrote this: "Often the difference between a successful person and one who fails is not who has the better abilities or ideas, but the one with the courage to bet on those ideas. And to act on them."

I love this quote because it opens so many doors for anyone who is willing to work hard and think outside the box.

———

Recognizing the abilities that you possess is the first step,
no doubt about it. And honing those abilities is an absolute must.
But trusting those abilities enough to take a chance on the new
and the different is what separates you from the rest of the field.

———

So while most of my friends stayed close to home and went back across the bridge to Mercer Island every other weekend, I took a bus south to the campus of Oregon State University, home of the Beavers, where I knew exactly one person. I could either make new friends and expand my horizons or I could hide out in my dorm room for four years. That didn't sound too appealing.

As if that wasn't enough, my parents decided to make my life even more interesting when they suddenly pulled up stakes from the great northwest and moved lock, stock, and barrel to San Rafael, just outside of San Francisco. Just like that, the support system I had back home had relocated 700 miles to the south. And just like that, the town of Corvallis was to be my home for the next four or so years, sink or swim. It was actually a good feeling.

Getting Out the Vote

The new morality of the 60s and 70s didn't really make its way onto the OSU campus, at least not while I was there. The word conservative hardly described the atmosphere there. So while college campuses from New England to sunny California were bursting at the seams with protest and political discourse over the war, civil rights, and gender discrimination, no one in their right mind at OSU would even consider staging a protest rally or burning their bras. Civil disobedience was a foreign concept.

But even the ultra-conservative outlook in Corvallis could not deny the revelations of the 26th Amendment, passed on July 1, 1971, giving every 18-year-old in the nation the right to vote.

I was stoked. If I couldn't get 20,000 students to burn their bras, I could at least get them to exercise their rights. That summer, Jim Wiggett and I went to the County Courthouse and applied to become Deputy Registrars so we could officially register students all over campus to vote.

Here was my chance to make a difference. Here was a chance to put the verb in the word leadership, though I wasn't really thinking of it like that back then. But I did think to myself: I can do this. I knew that most of the kids on campus would sign up, but I also knew that most of them would not go out of their way to do so. So I went to them. *Leadership = Taking Action.*

For the next four months, Jim and I spent pretty much every spare moment we had registering an entirely new voting population. And by the end of the year, we had signed up more new voters than anyone else in the entire state of Oregon.

I don't tell this story as a way of boasting, but only as a way of demonstrating how a 21-year-old can make a difference if he or she is willing to step out of the main- stream and risk failing.

As it turned out, my voter registration campaign ended up being one of the most fulfilling ventures of my college career, and I know it gave me the confidence to pursue other equally tenuous ventures later on.

The Road Trip

You know how some dates just seem to stick with you? Probably because the events or people attached to that date have a lasting effect on your life, even if you don't recognize it at the time.

February 18, 1971 was one of those dates for me. It didn't hurt that the next day was my twenty-first birthday, but that's not what led to the events in question. On that particular Thursday, my fraternity brother Dave Beeman and I were walking back across campus toward our fraternity house. It was the last day of midterms, and we had a long weekend ahead of us. The weather was typical of Corvallis that time of year, meaning cold, dreary, and perpetually damp. In a word: miserable. After four months of winter, Dave and I were sick of it.

"We need some sun," I said.

"You won't get any argument from me," Dave was quick to agree. "What do you have in mind?"

"Time for a road trip. South to California. We'll take my car," I said. "If we hit the road right now, we can make it to my parents' place in San Rafael by midnight."

"Say no more. I'm in."

In those days, I drove an MGB. After throwing toothbrushes and a change of clothes into a gym bag – so much for packing – Dave and I were in the car and headed south less than an hour later. I called my folks to tell them that two frat rats in need of a vacation were headed their way, and they promised a hot meal and two warm beds when we arrived. Sure enough, we were sitting across from my Dad – Dave with a beer in his hand and me with my signature Coke – by 11:00 and, thanks to Mom, well fed by midnight.

Lo and behold, we woke up the next morning, and it was still raining.

My Dad came into our room and broke the bad news. "Happy birthday, son. Get out your umbrellas."

Dave and I rolled out of bed. Here it was my twenty-first birthday, and the sun was nowhere to be seen. That wouldn't do. We hadn't driven all this way to sit out another rainstorm; we could have done that back in Corvallis. Undeterred, we bade Dad and Mom goodbye, gassed up the MGB, and hit the road again.

"Say hello to Connie for us," was the last thing Mom said.

Connie was my cousin and a junior at the University of California at Santa Barbara. Eight hours later, we were sitting on her front porch in Goleta basking in the late afternoon sun: mission accomplished.

"You're 21. It's time to party," Dave said, once the sun was down. In Corvallis, "time to party" generally meant a night out in one of the town's three taverns. A tavern in ultra-conservative Corvallis served wine and beer and featured an array of pool tables, Foosball tables, and pinball machines. The advantage to having only three taverns in a college town was the guarantee of knowing they would be packed every night of the week and overflowing on the weekends. Our favorite, a place called Goofy's, sold beer for 10 cents a glass. Too bad I didn't drink.

"Give us a tour, Connie," I said. "What's the hottest tavern in town?"

She looked at me as if I'd just broken into a foreign language and asked, "What's a tavern?"

"You know. A place where everyone goes for a beer and some music," I said.

"And maybe even to meet someone of the opposite sex," Dave added hopefully.

"Oh, well, the Holiday Inn on the edge of town has a band in the lounge on Friday and Saturday nights. But that's about it." She wasn't kidding.

I was shocked. But I was also inspired. There were 20,000 college kids at UCSB and not one bona fide tavern in which to hang out. A guy could make a killing.

I made up my mind right then and there to return to Goleta after graduation and to open a first-rate tavern catering to college-aged kids. I was already picturing the place. I could imagine the interior, picture the bar and the dance floor, and hear the music. I could also hear the cash register ringing.

——

I had a vision. It didn't scare me. I didn't think about the cost or the red tape. I didn't think about the zoning or the marketing. I told myself those things would take care of themselves. I had a vision, and I could picture it working.

——

There is a saying: "Man cannot discover new oceans unless he has the courage to lose sight of the shore."

I think about those words now and wonder if courage and feeling no fear are the same things. If so, I was on the right track.

Chapter 2

How Your Actions Become Habits

The Next Step

I always ask myself, "What's the next step?"

How do you get from the seed of an idea to the implementation of the idea and from a vague notion to slam-dunk success? By jumping off the bridge. How else? By grabbing hold of the notion of take-action leadership.

So when it came to this far-fetched notion I had about opening a nightclub in Goleta, I didn't just fantasize about it. I went back to OSU and wrote a thesis paper about it for one of my business courses. The paper covered every aspect of building a business from the ground floor up, using the opening of a hypothetical tavern in a college town as my subject.

The paper touched on location, theme, start-up costs, target audience, marketing, licensing: the works. It was 28 pages dedicated to an idea I was sure would work. That, in and of itself, was strong motivation. I got an "A" on the paper, and then put it aside. I still had a year of school ahead of me and a degree in Business Management to earn. But the idea wasn't forgotten; it was just stored away in some corner of my already cluttered mind.

After graduation, I took a detour, somewhat unintentionally following in my father's footsteps. Dad spent a good part of his career as a food broker and made a good living doing it. A food broker is basically a salesman who acts as an intermediary between food producers and food sellers, mostly grocery stores.

A college buddy of mine, Bill Campbell, had gotten a job in Los Angeles as an accountant with the Armour Meat Company. He was looking for a roommate. L.A. had always fascinated me, I suppose, but you don't get very far in the City of Angels without a job.

We got an apartment. He went to work, and I went looking. A newspaper ad led me to a company called Bradshaw Food Brokers. All of a sudden, I found myself going from grocery store to grocery story selling Bumble Bee Honey. I was making $800 a month and living hand to mouth like so many other 22-year-old college graduates.

The question then became: Now what? For one thing, I began to realize that everything I did today would reflect on the person I would be tomorrow. This realization led to a saying that I often use these days when speaking to young people about the business of life:

Watch your thoughts, for they become words.
Watch your words, for they become actions.
Watch your actions, for they become habits.
Watch your habits, for they become character.
Watch your character, for it becomes your destiny.

This may sound a bit lofty for a guy just out of college, but the truth of the matter is this: the habits you develop begin taking shape very early in life. The sooner you're aware of them – good or bad – the more clearly your character as a man or woman evolves and the more control you have over that evolution.

If you boil it down, your habits really do determine who you are on a daily basis. Your habits are what people see as you navigate the nuts and bolts of day-to-day living. Suddenly, you're staring the rest of your life in the face, and you hope you've built a strong foundation from which to work.

As I have said, I was a jumping-off-the-bridge kind of guy even back then and was about to prove it once again.

I met a girl named Janie Wood a couple of months into my L.A. hiatus, and we decided to spend a weekend away from the big city. I still had my trusty MGB, and we headed north without a real destination in mind. The further north we went, the closer we got to Santa Barbara. All of a sudden, I found myself thinking about my "building a business" thesis. I told Janie about my dream of opening my own tavern and realized it was a dream I had never given up on.

That night, we rented a room in a motel on the edge of town. The motel was across the street from a strip mall. There was a space for rent next to the local post office and a real estate agent's name in the window. The next morning, I said, "What the heck," picked up the phone and called the guy, just like that.

My line: "I'm thinking about opening up a tavern, and I'm looking for a building." Sure, it was a total crock on the one hand. But, on the other hand, it came down to the age-old saying: nothing ventured, nothing gained. I had a dream. I had to start somewhere.

The real estate agent took me at my word. He said, "Mr. Huntington, I've got just the building for you."

"Show me."

He did. Janie and I followed him into town, and we stopped in a large parking lot in front of a freestanding building with a wooden façade and a For Rent sign in the window. My heart was already pounding.

"It's 4,000 square feet and fully equipped. You could move in tomorrow," the agent said as he led us inside. I don't know what I was expecting. Probably a barren warehouse in need of a seasoned carpenter and a large expense account, but it was anything but. The space was already furnished with tables and chairs. A mahogany bar stretched across the back wall. We toured a walk-in cooler and a small kitchen. The agent was right: the place was ready to go.

He said, "You can probably tell that the building is already zoned for a restaurant and bar, so that's one hurdle you wouldn't have to clear." What he didn't say, and what I wouldn't find out until much later, was that the building had gone through 10 renters in 10 years. Not a good omen.

But I was 22 and far too naïve to figure out that it wouldn't work. I was making $800 a month and had a whopping $200 in the bank. I didn't care. My dream was starting to feel real.

Then came the big question, and the only one that really mattered: Where was I going to get the money?

Focus on What Matters

I will admit that I am an extremely conservative man when it comes to politics. I look at what our forefathers wrote down in the Bill of Rights and the US Constitution and think: Those guys had it right. We need to honor their vision.

But when it comes to taking a risk, most people would probably characterize me as a flaming liberal. Not true.

————

Here's my rule of thumb: You never jump without a plan. Bold is not the same as reckless.

————

Plato once said, "An unexamined life isn't worth living." His student, a guy named Aristotle, went further, saying, "An unplanned life isn't worth examining."

They were both talking about the same thing. Unless you have a plan for your life, you won't know what you're trying to accomplish. In other words, if you don't know what matters, it makes it hard to focus on what matters. That's my interpretation.

I got a heavy dose of this reality my senior year at Oregon State, when I served as a student member on the Athletic Department's Board of Directors. That was a group of bona fide heavy hitters who took the matters of OSU athletics very seriously. It was actually a position of some power for me because the Athletic Department was swimming in money, and the student board members had an equal say with faculty members and alumni members.

These men and women were some of the most focused and dedicated I would ever come in contact with, and I absorbed as much from them as I possibly could, on matters of business, to be sure, but also on life in general.

Frank Ramsey was the most impressive of the lot, and he treated me like a protégé. Frank was a huge man. He measured 6'4" and not a pound under 320, a force to be reckoned with. Frank was a member of the OSU 1942 Rose Bowl team, and the 1945 Chicago Cubs. He parlayed his notoriety into an extraordinary business career. Straight off the front lines in World War II, he bought some used logging equipment from the military and made his first fortune. Then he used his connections with legendary OSU football coach Tommy Prothro to obtain the franchise for the Oregon and Northern California Coca-Cola Bottling Company. Frank was easily the richest man in Corvallis.

I tussled with Frank over any number of issues concerning the athletic department – after all, I was a student and students didn't exactly look at things in the same way as those folks who woke up every morning and trudged off to earn a living – but Frank never took offense. In fact, I think he kind of admired my spunk.

I ran into Frank at a wedding reception my senior year, and he pulled me aside. He put an arm around my shoulders and said, "Craig, you're a good kid. If you ever need any dough, give me a call."

I don't know if Frank expected me to take him at his word, but I did. But not before I pulled out my thesis on "building a business" and updated it to reflect the nightclub in Santa Barbara. Before I was done, it looked like a professionally written business plan with all the numbers, all the paperwork, and a sales pitch worthy of an aspiring entrepreneur.

Then I contacted my good friend Steve Miller. Steve had graduated in Landscape Design and was working at Boxer Marcus, a large restaurant supply company in Portland. Steve was a talented artist. I asked him to design the club both inside and out, and his renderings were impressive. The name on the marquee out front read: F.U.B.A.R.

I called up Frank and asked for an audience. He said, "Come on up and we'll have breakfast. Meet me at the Town and Country Motel restaurant at 8:30."

Passion is What Makes the Plan

Frank may have said, "If you ever need any dough, call me up," but I knew even back then that it wasn't as simple as that. I had one opportunity to make my pitch and to convince him that putting his "dough" in a tavern was a good investment.

The Town and Country Motel was the best accommodation Corvallis had to offer in 1973. Like most small town motels across the country, the Town and Country wasn't particularly fancy. It had two stories of drive-up rooms with a café for breakfast and lunch. On one side of the café, there was an accordion door that they pushed aside every evening at 5:00 to access the "dining room." Back then, the Town and Country dining room was one of the best places for dinner in the entire town. When I arrived, I told the hostess I was meeting Frank Ramsey. She pointed to the accordion wall and said, "Right this way."

The hostess led me past the curtain into the dining room. There was Frank. He was sitting all alone in the middle of the restaurant at a table for six, reading the newspaper. He was the only person in the place.

The big man saw me and called, "Craig. Get over here. Good to see you."

Frank stood up, and we shook hands. "Thanks for seeing me," I said.

This was where Frank breakfasted every morning, he and whomever he invited for an audience. I was scared to death, full of enthusiasm, and brimming with excitement. I laid my business plan and renderings on the table, but Frank didn't so much as glance at them. "Let's eat something," he said.

We ordered breakfast, and I gave him my pitch. I was all over the map with my thoughts, but there was no mistaking the passion I had for the idea. As it turned out, Frank never did look at my business plan or Steve's drawings. I realized that was probably a good thing.

———

He told me later that it was my passion for the project that sold him, and that the project's success would hinge on that passion. He was right. Without passion, all the planning in the world is meaningless.

———

"So how much dough do you need?" Just like that, sipping his coffee, and mopping his plate with a piece of toast.

"I need $10,000." Ten thousand wasn't near enough, but what did I know about the real world. The building's owner wanted $4,500 right off the top: $1,500 for the first and last month's rent and a $1,500 deposit. I had no product, no license, and no hired help.

"Okay, fine. Here's the deal," Frank said. "We'll each pony up $2,000. Then we'll get a $6,000 loan from Bank of America. We'll set up a corporation. I'll get my lawyers to draw it up. I'll own 51% and you'll own 49%. We'll call it HunRam (Huntington and Ramsey) Enterprises. Clever, huh? And then we'll build this thing."

"Okay, Frank. Thanks." We shook hands. It was as simple as that.

Then it got complicated. I needed to raise $2,000. First, I sold my MGB for $1,500 and used $500 of that to buy myself a serious clunker. I was halfway there. I went to my dad for the other thousand, and he turned me down.

"You can't do this," he said. "You'll never make it."

That hurt. But it also motivated me. No way I was going to fail. I made my pitch to a dozen different people. My best friend, Dave Peoples, lent me $500, and a friend of my dad's, Walter Turner, co-signed on a credit card with a $500 advance. I had my two grand.

I started lining up contacts for food and alcohol, phone and electricity, rentals for pool tables and pinball machines. Everything. I wanted to be ready to go the minute we had our $6,000 loan in hand.

I went to Frank and told him where things stood. He called up his banker at the Bank of America in San Francisco. Grady Rutledge happened to be working on a $900,000 loan for Frank at the same time, so $6,000 was like pocket change.

"Grady, call your branch in Goleta and tell them to draw up a $6,000 loan. I'll have my partner go in to open up an account," I heard him say.

The bank was only a half-mile from the tavern, so I walked from there. I went inside, and the lady in the loan department got the application together and then informed me that she would need Frank's financial statements, tax returns, and so on.

I couldn't believe it. I wanted to say, "Ma'am, this is Frank Ramsey, one of your biggest depositors. Are you kidding?" But I didn't. I walked back to the club and used the pay phone – no, I didn't have phone service yet – to call Frank.

Frank was furious. "I'm not sending the bank in Goleta a damn thing." Or words to that effect; Frank had a very colorful vocabulary. "You go back there and tell that ***** woman to call Grady Rutledge and get that ***** loan done."

That was Frank. An artist had once drawn a caricature of the big guy that hung in his office behind his desk: huge head, feet up on the desk, cigar in mouth, phone in hand. The picture showed a tiny guy talking to Frank from a phone in Japan. The guy was saying, "Frank, they won't do the deal." And Frank snarls, "Then buy the whole ***** island." That was how Frank worked.

I went back to the bank, but the lady refused to call Grady Rutledge. She said, "No financials, no $6,000. Period." Now I was getting worried.

I had bills to pay and a club to open. The building's owner was waiting on my deposit.

No Excuses

I had a dilemma. I had kicked the rock down the mountain. And I had, as a consequence, done exactly what we were discussing in Chapter One: Take Action…Now.

That being said, the situation I was facing also brought into perspective a mindset that having passion for an idea naturally generates:

- **Have no excuses.**
- **Refuse to believe in limits.**
- **Think before you react.**

I took these three rules in reverse order. I knew I didn't want to call Frank back and confess to another failed meeting. I also decided I couldn't let one woman without a lick of common sense squelch my dreams. If I used that as an excuse, I would never be able to look myself in the mirror again.

This is how many bankers are today and were back then: thinking out of the box is a foreign concept. Too many bankers are reactive, not proactive, and anything that doesn't fit into their preordained set of rules is a no-no.

Still, calling Frank back took every ounce of courage I could muster, and his reaction was predictable. "Who the ***** is this woman?"

Frank sent me straight back to the bank. "I'll make a call," he said.

He called Grady Rutledge, who called the loan officer and essentially said, "I'm working on a $900,000 deal here and you're screwing around with six thousand. Get it done."

I walked into the bank for the third time that day, and the greeting I received this time around was like night and day. "Right this way, Mr. Huntington. So good to see you. Would you like the entire $6,000 deposited into your checking account, or is there some other arrangement we can make?"

The bank treated me like royalty from that day forward, and I got the club cranked up. But my learning curve would prove to be a steep one. I made my first big mistake when I walked into the Santa Barbara Franchise Tax Board to apply for my business license.

First question: "How much business are you anticipating per month, Mr. Huntington?"

For some reason, I felt it was important to make an impression. I wanted to live up to my over-inflated projections and, of course, I had my ego to satisfy. I said, "I'm planning on doing $50,000 per month."

I had no idea they were going to use that number to estimate my taxes, nor that I was expected to pay three months in advance. I stared at the bill: $3,900.

I could have said I was planning on making $5,000 per month, and the deposit would have been $390. But the moral of the story is that I wasn't prepared. I hadn't done my research, and I wasn't being realistic.

Passion is a good thing, make no mistake about it; however, there are times when you need to keep it in check.

———

A wise man once said, "Success comes when preparation meets opportunity." Being prepared may sound like a Boy Scout motto, but it fits the business world like a glove.

———

After paying my landlord $4,500, I now had $1,600 left in my bank account, and I hadn't even opened my doors yet.

By this time, I had given up my apartment in L.A. and was sleeping on a pool table in the club. Every morning I would jump into my five-hundred-dollar-clunker, drive to the UCSB campus, and sneak into the gym to shower and shave. I was living on a shoestring, but the adrenaline was pumping 24/7. I was days away from opening my own business and couldn't have been more excited.

I called the club F.U.B.A.R., military slang for F***ed Up Beyond All Recognition. I was 23. I thought the name was as clever as could be. We opened on a Friday night in October of 1973, beer and wine only.

Because no distributor in his right mind would issue credit to a 23-year-old first-time club owner, all deliveries were cash on the barrelhead. I had six shipments coming that day and wrote six bad checks. By then, the $10,000 was gone. I had spent every penny outfitting the interior and advertising opening night. *Please, God, make it successful.*

I had eight people on staff and a live band. The people swarmed the place from all over Santa Barbara. I was ecstatic and overwhelmed. Here I was running a tavern with no experience and no clue. All I had was unabashed passion for the idea and complete confidence in myself.

Thinking on Your Feet

This is not a cliché. It is a piece of a very important puzzle that can spell the difference between success and failure.

- **You begin with a plan.**
- **You evolve a strategy, and then implement the strategy.**
- **You hire good people and let them do their job.**
- **You allow yourself to make mistakes, and you learn from them.**
- **You think on your feet.**

We made a cool $2,000 that first night, and did even better that Saturday. I hadn't planned on live music for that Sunday night, and business tanked.

———

**I learned. You'd better not expect the business to come to you.
Give them the best product available, and then give
them something extra. Don't cut corners.
In other words, have a hook, but make certain
the hook has substance.**

———

So I got creative. Tuesday nights became "Ten cent beer night." We sold beer for 10 cents a glass from 7:30 to 9:30, and had live music from 9:00 until close. Live music meant a cover charge.

Wednesday featured our wet t-shirt contest (remember, this was the 70s, and gimmicks like that worked in the 70s).

Thursday was Ladies' Night. Girls got in free, and girls were a must if you were going to be successful in the nightclub business.

Friday and Saturday, live music from 9:00 until close, and I was bringing in bands from all over California.

Every night, the doors were open to girls over 18 and guys over 21. I know how that sounds, but you could get away with things like that back then. It was a marketing ploy, and it worked wonders.

Within a month, F.U.B.A.R. grew to become the hottest club from Calabasas to San Luis Obispo. I paid off our loan. I rented an apartment. I bought a new car. I'd driven down the road of risk and made my dream a reality.

Chapter 3

Just Do It – A Habit, Not a Cliché

He Who Character Perseveres

For five years, I made a lot of money running F.U.B.A.R.

Five years was a good run in the nightclub business. Of course, I was young and didn't know what to do with the money. I spent it as fast as I made it. I had to have a Porsche. I had to have a phone in my Porsche, and a car phone was an expensive affair in the 70s. It didn't work worth a damn, but I was cool. I'd take off at a moment's notice and travel across the country. I bought a condo; and buying Santa Barbara real estate turned out to be the only smart thing I did with my money.

Unfortunately, I didn't have anyone I could look to for prudent financial counsel, but I'm not sure I would have listened had someone stepped forward.

I felt like I was doing things my way. That was a good thing for the most part.

I felt like I was willing to travel down roads that not just anyone would go down. I felt like I was willing to take risks even though I hadn't thought out every angle, every contingency, or every pitfall.

———

I said earlier that planning is an important part of living well.
It is necessary in conducting business successfully.
There is no way you can predict the future.
There is no way you can completely mitigate
the possibility of failure.

———

There are times when you just have to take the leap. Not just in business, but in your personal life as well. What does this mean? It means pursuing relationships that might seem risky; making choices that might seem difficult; thinking out of the box just because life is too short not to crash and burn every once in a while.

The Man Who Refused to Quit:

Perseverance

He failed in business in 1831.
He was defeated for state legislator in '32.
He tried another business in '33. It failed.
His fiancée died in '35.
He had a nervous breakdown in '36.
In '43 he ran for Congress and was defeated.
He tried again in '48 and was defeated again.
He tried running for the Senate in '55. He lost.
The next year he ran for Vice President and lost.
In '59 he ran for the Senate again and was defeated.
In 1860, the man who signed his name A. Lincoln,
was elected the 16th president of the United States of America.

———

The difference between history's boldest accomplishments and its most staggering failures is often, simply, the diligent will to persevere.

———

Can you imagine if our sixteenth President had given up in 1848 after losing for the second time in his run for Congress?

Can you imagine if he had said, "Public service isn't for me. I'm going back to Kentucky and becoming a blacksmith."?

Can you imagine how different our country would be today?

Lincoln is a great example, but the truth is, we can all think of people who refused to give up when the going got tough. People who refused to throw in the towel after falling short or failing.

Picking yourself up after you fall is just another form of taking action. Do it often enough and it becomes a habit.

Defining Your Character

We talked about how your actions become your habits over time. We talked about how your habits define your character, and how being aware of your character steers you toward your destiny. This very comforting thought is, in many ways, a roadmap, and cultivating a "Just Do It" habit can make all the difference in the road you eventually travel down.

Yes, we all attribute the "Just Do It" motto to Nike, and there is a message in the motto we shouldn't ignore. "Just Do It" is not a reckless statement. It doesn't imply doing crazy things just to fit in or for the sake of pure adrenaline. What is does imply is a willingness to identify your dreams – big, small, or otherwise – and to commit yourself to chasing them, even if it does lead to some rejection or disappointment or failure. At least you're living. And the upside is that it may also lead to things like success, illumination, and satisfaction.

I went into the bar business to make money. I didn't drink, so it wasn't that. And the fact of the matter is, a lot of people are in the bar business because of the alcohol. I didn't indulge in drugs. In fact, I was anti-drug to the point of banning marijuana and cocaine from the premises.

I played by the rules. I didn't alienate the community. I worked closely with the police. I wanted them on my side in case there was ever any trouble, and there was always a certain amount of trouble in the tavern business.

But working for the money is only good as long as the passion and the commitment remain: the passion and the commitment for the enterprise, for the pursuit of whatever goals you have set, and for the fulfillment of the dream.

**In the business world, you have to be willing to reinvent yourself.
You have to be willing to adjust your strategy and
retool your tactics. Change is the only constant,
in some businesses more than others.**

The nightclub business fit the latter more than most; it was a continuous process of reinventing the model, and 18 to 30-year-olds are the most fickle of all clients. The latest club is always the club of choice.

The era of disco arrived, and F.U.B.A.R. was a rock 'n roll club. In 1978, I sold the club for probably more than it was worth – though hardly a fortune – and opened a discotheque halfway between Oxnard and Ventura. I was ready for a change.

The "Think Different" Habit

My twenties turned out to be an opportunity to invest in my future, and I didn't do it.

This is not to say that the steps I was taking in establishing a bona fide "think different" habit weren't positive. They were. At the age of 23, I had opened a groundbreaking rock 'n roll club where few like it had existed before. I came away from the venture with a wealth of street sense, an understanding of the bottom line, and no shortage of confidence. But what I had not come away with was much in the way of real wealth. I could have invested 20% or 25% of what I was making, in particular over the course of the first three or four years of the business, socked it away and allowed time to work in my favor. The money would have been worth a fortune today.

I didn't have anyone in my life preaching such prudent investing, and I might not have listened anyway. But I did learn enough over the years to preach a similar lesson to my own kids. They've heard this or something similar since before they got out of middle school: From the day you start working, put 10% of your paycheck into some kind of interest-bearing asset. Ten per cent every month. Just do it. Make a habit of it. And down the road, the habit will pay you back in multiples beyond your wildest dreams.

I didn't get that message; few from my generation did.

But despite my inclination to spend everything I made back then, I was on my way to establishing two habits straight from our "Leadership is a Verb" credo: A "think different" habit and a "just do it" habit.

I had no real world experience when it came to opening F.U.B.A.R. I didn't know the difference between white wine and red wine, or a dark beer from a light one. Yet I got by on hard work, perseverance, and passion.

F.U.B.A.R. was a 120-hour-a-week proposition, and the hours didn't faze me for a second. I was building something. I would wake up in the morning – sometimes with less than four hours' sleep – and be excited by what the new day had to offer.

———

I believe that if you're truly passionate about something, that something is, for no other reason, truly important. The two go hand in hand.

———

This is not to criticize or denigrate the man or woman who chooses a steady 9 to 5, Monday through Friday, job. This is not to say that their choice of employment, career, or vocation inspires any less passion than the entrepreneur who jumps off the bridge and follows a path littered with pitfalls and potential failure. This may be someone who goes to the beach with his or her family on weekends or has dinner at home five nights a week. This may be someone who values predictability and security. In any case, a lust for life is as important as a passion for your profession is. Otherwise, why do it?

My brother Brent is a great example. He works as an electrician. He's a 9 to 5 guy. He's good at what he does, but he doesn't obsess about the job once he clocks out. He goes fishing as often as he can. He takes his sailboat out whenever the weather permits. He rarely works weekends. For all I know, he'll probably outlive me by 20 years. He's chosen his path; I've chosen mine. Neither is better than the other. The key is in the choosing and making the most of your choice. Brent has done that. So have I.

Here is another Craig-ism I have often shared with my kids: It's both the guys in the paneled offices on the top floor and the night janitor that make a company work. Every person in every enterprise has a part to play.

———

If you go to bed happy and wake up happy, it doesn't matter what that part is.

———

Are You Experienced?

We've all heard it a hundred times, and we all come to realize how true it is: experience is the best teacher.

My continuing experience came when I met a neurosurgeon (a good guy who will remain nameless here) who, as luck would have it, had tried to open a nightclub 40 miles south of Santa Barbara in the city of Oxnard. The club had gone belly up. The doc had lost his shirt, and the building had been gathering dust for months.

I was on the hunt for a new venture, and he was willing to hand over the operation to someone with more experience and more time. We agreed on a 50-50 partnership. My 50% was essentially sweat equity, roll up my sleeves and get in there and make the place work. His 50% called for an influx of new capital, but the money he agreed to put up was not sufficient.

Mistake #1: Being Under-Capitalized is a Killer

Being under-capitalized is as bad as misappropriating the capital that you have. It puts you behind the eightball even before you start.

Yes, I spent the money we had wisely, but I knew it wasn't enough to compete in the "glitz and glamour" world of disco, where show was often just as important as substance: the sunken dance floor, the strobes and the blue lights, the high-end sound system, the high-priced DJ.

Youth still being one of my primary problems, I thought I could beat the odds. I remodeled. I advertised. I paid off the fire department so they would sign off on my building. And on January 1, 1978, I opened Huntington's Dining and Disco. We opened with a good crowd that was never destined to be a great crowd, not in Oxnard.

Mistake #2: Location, Location, Location

The demographics killed me, right from the get-go. Huntington's Dining and Disco was located on the border between Oxnard and Ventura, within view of the Santa Clara River. I was expecting to draw from the more affluent crowd in Ventura, and failed to realize that the beach community that made the town famous refused to set foot in middle class Oxnard.

You've heard the saying "On the wrong side of the tracks." Well, Huntington's was on the wrong side of the river, literally. Had the new club been located a stone's throw away on the other side of the Santa Clara, it would have been a whole different story.

The location issue also posed another problem, above and beyond the clientele we were attracting. Unlike Santa Barbara, the community in Oxnard never fully embraced the club. Despite my best efforts, the police were not on my side, therefore they were less visible, which meant there was more trouble.

My point is that you can never foresee every obstacle to a new venture, try as you might. If you expect to have every contingency covered or think you'll be able to anticipate every pitfall, you'll never muster the courage to take the Y down the road called risk.

Risks are inherent in everything we do. Thinking different insures you'll make mistakes, but the man or woman who thinks out of the box rebounds from his or her mistakes and turns them into positives.

———

Here's the key point that often eludes us. You're responsible for every decision you make. Circumstances, bad luck, misfortune, or folly are not worthy excuses for failure, any more than booming economic times, good luck, or good fortune are explanations for success. It's the actions you take.

———

Back when F.U.B.A.R.'s explosive business began to wane, I blamed "changing times" for the decline. The problem was, I was to blame. The strategy I was employing (or not employing) left the club unprepared for the changing times. I was so enamored with our short-term success that I failed to prepare for the long term and to anticipate the really revolutionary changes that disco would have on the club scene.

This brings up another fundamental issue. It's difficult to cash in on a fad – no matter what industry you're in – unless you strike early, have luck on your side, and go in with a sure-fire exit strategy. Disco, in my case, was a fad. My expertise was the rock 'n roll scene, the bar scene. I understood that audience. With Huntington's, I strayed from my expertise and created a product that was only marginally successful. It was far from a failure, but it didn't meet my definition of success.

Knowing Your Strengths is a Strength

I discovered that one of my strengths is building something from the ground up.

I am not as effective in the actual running of the operation once the business is established.

I am extremely focused on creating strategy.

I am not as effective when it comes to the tactical aspects of carrying out the strategy.

No problem. Except for the fact that I had not actually sat down and identified those strengths and weaknesses back then.

**Identifying your strengths and your weaknesses
cannot – or should not – be an exercise in hindsight.
It should be an ongoing process.**

I have at least learned enough about this to encourage the people who work for me now to sit down with a piece of paper and to create two lists:

What I do well.

What I don't do well.

How do you start? It's really not that difficult. Think about the things that you enjoy. I enjoy public speaking; it's a strength. I don't care for accounting; numbers aren't a strength. I'm an entrepreneur and a big picture guy; I love to get things rolling. I'm not a detail guy; I get bored easily. I love rock 'n roll. I don't care for disco. And that's probably one reason Huntington's only lasted four years and wasn't as successful as F.U.B.A.R.

It's very likely that you'll be successful doing the things that you enjoy. After all, enjoyment is a byproduct of passion, and passion is a key component in living successfully.

Proactive as a Way of Life

Even though Huntington's Dining and Disco faced its share of uphill obstacles – location, under-capitalization, and timing chief among them – what never waned was my eagerness to explore a new enterprise and my willingness to throw 100% of my energy into it. The obstacles actually motivated me. I bought out my partner, closed the dining room, and focused on entertainment.

We were never in the red. We paid our bills, and I was able to take some profits. I viewed that as a measure of success given the circumstances. But after three years, I saw the writing on the wall. I could see that disco was going to have a short life span, so I started to plan an exit strategy.

Expanding Horizons

It wasn't a lack of satisfaction or an overabundance of unfulfilled hours in the day that got me thinking about the new venture I was about to embark on. I was just in the right place at the right time. But being in the right place at the right time is not coincidence or happenstance; it's a product of taking action and being active.

So three years after opening Huntington's, I started my own property management company, and a new phase in my business life began.

The story began when I decided to purchase a condo in a small, 80-unitcomplex called Cabrillo Park Condominiums. Exercising a constant need to be involved, I decided to attend the homeowners association annual meeting. This was the meeting where everyone got together, voiced their various complaints, and elected the association's five-member Board of Directors.

I was 29 at the time, and the complex was filled with an eclectic mix of people old and young. There were families, retirees, singles, very much in line with the demographics of a middle-income community.

The association meeting was a rowdy affair that allowed the residents to voice their concerns about the management company that handled the affairs of the complex, things like collecting tenant fees and coordinating trash pickup, building maintenance, and landscaping, all of the things that most of the occupants took for granted. And since it was the Board that hired the management company, the homeowners also used the meeting to voice their opinions about the Board and to make changes if they saw fit.

At one point, an old guy jumped up and said, "What about those damn teenagers who keep taking over the Jacuzzi and the pool? Raising hell and splashing water all over hell and gone. Something's got to be done."

"The noise is something awful," a woman with a baby in her arms said. "I can't even take my kids down there."

This got the rest of the crowd up in arms. "The pool used to be the kind of place where my wife and I could go to relax, but we don't even bother any more," another guy hollered. "And I want to know what the board is going to do about it."

On and on it went until I finally raised my hand and stood up. "Why don't you just grab them by their long hair, pull them out of the pool, and throw them out on their ears? Pretty simple. I don't understand the problem."

Of course, that was easy for me to say. I came from the nightclub business where a bouncer was worth his weight in gold. Troublemakers were literally tossed out the front door, down a flight of concrete stairs, and told not to come back. That was how things were handled in the 70s. And the police were completely sympathetic, at least they had been at F.U.B.A.R. in Santa Barbara. My rationale was that if it worked at the nightclub, it would surely work with a handful of rowdy teenagers.

Everyone in the meeting just stared at me. Then the old guy jumped up again and shouted, "I nominate Mr. Huntington for the Board. All in favor."

Every hand in the room went up. It was unanimous. Here I was, 29-years-old and a member of the Cabrillo Park Board of Directors, a purely voluntary position that proved to be more involved than I could have ever anticipated.

Once a month, the board met with the complex's property management company to discuss ongoing matters related to the collection and expenditure of association fees. The management company was charged with seeing that the swimming pool was cleaned, the lawn was mowed, and the gardens were tended. They were also charged with enforcing the complex's rules. Pretty straightforward!

For the first meeting or two, I listened and learned. But keeping quiet was not my strong suit. You have to remember that I was a bottom line guy. I was used to running my own business, and I knew what a proper profit and loss statement was supposed to look like. I understood what things cost and when inefficiencies were getting in the way of a job well done. And it was becoming clear to me that our property management company could have been doing its job a whole lot better.

Since I didn't go into the nightclub until three or four in the afternoon most days, I also began fielding a lot of complaints from the other owners. The sprinklers were broken. The outside lights were on day and night. The trash was piling up. I started attending to problems that, by all rights, the property management company should have been attending to and doing a better job of it, to boot.

———

Here was another opportunity to demonstrate my as yet unwritten motto: Leadership is a verb. Take action.

———

So that was what I did. I went to my fellow board members and said, "I can do what our property management company is doing, and I can do it a lot better. I want their contract."

That was the start of Huntington Property Management.

Chapter 4

Awakening Leadership

Focus and Prioritize

I wasn't intimidated by the idea of running two businesses – the club and the property management company – at the same time. I also wasn't concerned by the obvious fact that running a nightclub and managing a condominium complex were, at least on the surface, like walking on two different planets. If I worked hard at both and smart at both, I could be successful at both.

I told myself from the beginning not to give less effort or time to one than the other, even while I was learning on the fly about the property management business.

This is where the concept of "focus and prioritize" took front and center.

My first task was to resign my position on the board, because a property manager serving on the board of a community he managed was a major conflict of interest.

I made it official when I went out and had a box of business cards printed up: Huntington Property Management, Craig Huntington, Owner/Operator. I registered the name. I got a tax ID number.

I settled into a schedule.

I went to the club every afternoon at 3:30. By that time, my day manager, Richard Singleton, had been there since 10:00. The place was clean, and the day's order of food and liquor had been received. Faxing food and liquor orders to our distributors was one of the last things I did after the club closed at 2:00 every morning. This guaranteed freshness and a minimum amount of waste. It also kept costs under control.

―――

Don't skimp, but don't get overextended either.

―――

If I was lucky, my head hit the pillow by 3:00; twelve hours on the job give or take, and I never gave it a thought. I was up by 8:00 and going full bolt on Huntington Property Management by 9:00.

Here's how the business worked. Cabrillo Park Condominiums consisted of 80 units. The average monthly homeowners fee was approximately $80. This $6,400 pie had to be sliced up to pay for everything from pool maintenance and landscaping to electrical bills and water. The property management company was responsible for collecting all these fees, paying all these bills, and for monitoring such things as the maintenance and the lawn mowing, among other things. Picture a trust. The management company is essentially the trustee in charge of looking out for the homeowners' best interest. For its trouble, the company receives $6.00 per unit management fee. In my case, this came to around $500.

I opened a bank account in the association's name.

It was my job to collect 80 checks from 80 homeowners and deposit them in the name of the association. In the short time I had spent observing how this property management stuff worked, I learned one thing quickly: NO ONE TRUSTS THE MANAGEMENT COMPANY. To help get past this perception, I approached a small local bank called Hacienda Federal Savings and Loan and asked them if I could have all the homeowners' checks sent directly to them instead of to me. By cutting the management company out of the money collection loop, I felt people would trust me more. I also thought it might save me a little time opening envelopes and making deposits. In return, I promised the bank that I would transfer all of the association's deposits – in this case, all $40,000 of it – into their bank. The bank agreed to this direct-deposit arrangement, and the "Lockbox," as it would come to be known, began in earnest.

———

Little did I know at the time, but this "Lockbox" idea would, in the not-too-distant-future, change my life.

———

My other duties with the homeowners association included writing the requisite checks for all monthly expenses, making sure any work that needed doing got done, and that any problems that might arise had solutions.

I was good at it. My experience in running F.U.B.A.R. and Huntington's Dining and Disco (less the dining) had given me a keen understanding of the bottom line and for balancing costs and revenue.

———

It doesn't matter whether your business is wildly successful or not; there are always lessons to be learned and tools you can develop to help you in whatever you're pursuing tomorrow or the next day or the day after that. A smart man doesn't hide from his mistakes. He doesn't overreact to his successes.

———

Michael Jordan once said, "I've failed over and over and over again in my life and that is why I succeed."

There may not be anything overly profound in that, except the realization that roadblocks are actually the building blocks of success. You learn to climb them, go around them, or go through them.

I really knew nothing about the property management business – at least I had never been schooled in it – but I had the audacity to believe that I could be wildly successful doing it. Property management was not high science; it did not require me to learn an entirely new skill set. I could see the steps that were necessary in doing the job right, and recognized the necessity of being organized about the day-to-day details of the condominium complex and being sensitive to the needs of the homeowners association. The less I heard from the board, the easier my job was.

From the outset, I realized that the responsibilities and time involved in managing Cabrillo Park did not balance well with the $500 I was putting in my pocket every month. How could I increase my take and make myself even more indispensable to the association? I saw myself writing a check for $1,400 every month to the guys mowing the lawn and tending the shrubs, and realized the way to make this new enterprise work was to accept more responsibility, not less. The landscaping was a cash cow. So was the swimming pool maintenance. I went to the board and said, "I want the landscaping contract, and I want to maintain the pool. Let's get all of these activities under one umbrella where I can control the quality and make everyone's lives a little easier."

I didn't say, "So I can reap the rewards," but that was the idea.

Why Take More Risk?

Here is a chart that has become a mainstay in my approach to the business world.

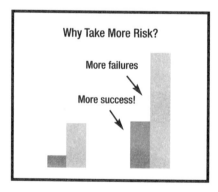

I imagine this is a chart that Michael Jordan would also approve of after reading his quote earlier in this chapter.

It's a simple ratio. Failures occur more often than successes. You have to be comfortable with failing in order to reap the rewards of success. You have to view failures as positive stepping-stones to success. The more risks you're willing to take, the more often you're going to succeed.

Unless you live in a bubble, you're going to make mistakes. You're going to experience failure and loss. That's life. The upside is the positives you create, the products you produce, the relationships that you build.

So here I was running a property management company. Every activity I was engaged in required the balancing of revenues generated against costs incurred: basic accounting. I'm not a numbers guy, but even I could see this.

The revenue was good, but not good enough. How could I make the budget work to my advantage without devaluing the quality of the product or damaging my relationship with the association?

I had a budget of $6,400. If I could manage the property and all of its needs for less than $6,400, I would be generating positive funds for the association without jeopardizing my fee. If I was generating positive funds for the association, I could profit as well by taking, say, 25% of savings in return. So that's what I proposed to the board. If I could manage their property without loss of quality for less than their monthly budget, I would invest 75% of any accrued savings in an interest bearing account with their bank, and take 25% for myself.

It was a win-win situation for everyone involved. This was an out-of-the-box idea. It was unique to the industry, and the board had no reason to refuse. They benefited. The association benefited. I benefited.

———

The key when it comes to thinking outofthebox is not to cut corners. Cutting corners undermines any creative thinking you might be trying to implement. It you can't do it the right way, then think of another way.

———

I had seen the negative effects of cutting corners at the disco, mostly because the funds just weren't there. And here's what I discovered: cutting corners is a self-perpetuating spiral that inevitably leads to further decline in the quality of the product.

With the property management company, I realized I was onto something special – a bona fide business – if I focused on doing the job like I knew it had to be done.

So the question arises: how do you grow a business?

Well, the very first thing so many people focus on is cutting expenses: "If we can cut costs, we can improve revenues." This is backward thinking. You don't take away a salesperson's ability to take a client to lunch, or cut staff in your customer service department, trying to save a buck. You grow a business by enhancing your services and creating cutting edge products. You differentiate; you don't downsize.

This is not to say that cutting waste or paring unproductive processes from an operation or a system isn't effective or necessary at times. But cutting just to save a penny here or a penny there at the expensive of motivation, creativity, or productivity is not the way to grow a business.

Small Steps, Big Results

I was into my third business, from rock 'n roll and disco to property management. As different as night and day, right? But here are a couple of common sense rules that work in the bar business as well as they do the world of homeowners associations.

Rule one: Never ignore the basics.
Rule two: You can't control everything.

So, with regard to my new property management business, I started with the basics in my efforts to maximize my budget. I began monitoring the electronically-controlled lights; if they were supposed to go on at 7:00, I made sure the clocks were set accordingly. I hired a local kid to help with the landscaping and began mowing the lawn myself (this was less like work than it seems since I happen to love mowing). I monitored the Jacuzzi, because a Jacuzzi uses up electricity faster than an SUV burns gas. I was able to drive our electric bill down from $1,000 per month to $700, and made $75 in the process. Efficiency became my best friend.

The term "focus and prioritize" took on added meaning every day. I was excited by the prospect of developing this entity called Huntington Property Management. It wasn't as flashy as the nightclub business, but it was an opportunity that got the blood pumping. It was an opportunity to make money – not an unimportant element with respect to a new enterprise – but taking the risk was equally important.

Walking the Walk

I worked the property management business with the same gusto I had F.U.B.A.R., and as I was doing with Huntington's Dining and Disco. I hired good help – a couple of young guys who were willing to work hard for a fair wage – but I also committed myself to the physical work as well.

———

For me, the best way to motivate your team is to show them that you're willing to get yourself dirty. For me, managers should never ask their staff to do anything they wouldn't do themselves.

———

Hard work is something I value because the results are so tangible. When you mow the lawn, you can see the results. Sure, you can give orders all day – and sometimes that's necessary – but personal production is something you can put your arms around.

It became clear to me, even as my understanding of the property management business grew more acute, that the real money was tied to managing multiple complexes. However, the opportunity came sooner than I expected.

I was having lunch with David Bowles, a good friend from my F.U.B.A.R. days, when we started discussing my new venture. This caught David's attention, because he lived in a 600-unit complex in Port Hueneme adjacent to the military base. These were small four-plex units that rented for maybe $400 per month. The complex was run by a typical homeowners association.

"And I think they're really screwing us, Craig," David said.

I shrugged. "Well, let's take a look at their books."

As a member of the association, David had every right to demand a review of the books, and it didn't take me long to see what a mess they were. Money was clearly being misused, if not intentionally, then through negligence. Worse yet, the President of the Board, a kindly, blue-haired lady of 75, was being paid by the management company to be their site manager, a clear-cut conflict of interest, primarily because *she* was approving *their* pay, and they were turning around and giving *her* a nice little stipend.

I could see from my own experience with Cabrillo Park that the waste of money, time, and resources was extraordinary at Port Hueneme. And it went well beyond that. Their association had $300,000 in the bank. Interest rates at the time – this being the Jimmy Carter era – were 16% and 17%. But the Port Hueneme association was not taking advantage of this. Their money was in passbook accounts earning a measly 3%, a remarkable example of mismanagement and/or incompetence.

With this ammunition available to us, David and I initiated a proxy takeover of the association's board. We sent out a letter to all the Port Hueneme homeowners, explaining the issues and asking each of them to sign a proxy giving David their vote at the next annual meeting. The response was overwhelming. Come the next meeting, David showed up with 420 votes, laid them on the table, and took over the home-owners association.

His first order of business was to hire Huntington Property Management to manage the complex's affairs. Suddenly, I was in charge of two condominium complexes and nearly 700 units.

Time to go into the business full time.

Chapter 5

The Power to Decide

A Circle Within a Circle

We are all concerned about the various influences that affect our lives.

We wake up in the morning wondering what the day's weather will look like. We're concerned about whether or not that bonus will be forthcoming, and if so, how big it will be. We think about the projects we're working on, the plane flight we have to make, the traffic, office politics, and what we should get our spouses for their birthdays. You've got your list. I've got mine. We all have them.

There is a wonderful concept developed by Stephen Covey in his book, *The Seven Habits of Highly Effective People*, that I often refer to when I'm speaking in front of people in my industry. He calls it our **Circle of Concern**: these are the items that muddle our thinking and steal our energy. Some of the matters within our circle are important, while plenty of others are insignificant and a waste of time. You know the ones I'm talking about.

However, within this "circle of concern," Mr. Covey also talks about our **Circle of Influence**.

Within this "circle of influence," there are any number of items that we actually have control over. These are items we can and should be focusing our attention on. What are these? The projects we're working on today. The relationships we're building today. Our state of mind. How we choose to react to events and people. Whom we choose to deal with day to day. The agenda for an upcoming sales meeting. The exercise program we decide to implement. Again, you have your list, and I have mine. The point is, these are the items in our lives that we have influence over.

Outside of this circle are the items like the state of the economy, the crime rate, the way people think or act. Yes, these items impact our lives to some degree, but we DO NOT have influence on them.

Understanding the difference between our "circle of concern" and our "circle of influence" is critical to our success and our happiness.

———

We want our circle of influence to grow. We accomplish this by having a proactive focus. We focus on what we can change, influence, and impact.

———

What is this "proactive focus" that we're talking about? This is when you focus on things you can influence. And when you do, you expand your knowledge and experience. You build skills and trustworthiness. As a result, your circle of influence grows.

Juxtapose this against what I call a "reactive focus." This very unproductive behavior occurs when you waste your time focusing on the items outside your circle of influence. And when that happens, your circle of influence shrinks. You become reactionary, allowing events and people that are outside of your control to overpower you and to sap your energy.

This is a terrible situation that can potentially affect everything in your life.

Ask yourself this question: How much time do you spend thinking about and worrying about items that are completely out of your control? It can be a very long list, especially with the increasingly hectic pace of our increasingly crazy world and the growing influence of modern technology.

The Don't Do List

So how do we control this impulse to worry about things we can't possibly control? How do we turn ourselves from a reactive mindset to a proactive one? My suggestion: A "Don't Do List."

This list looks just like the "To Do List" we all seem to write for ourselves most everyday. Now try writing down all the things you can't control and commit yourself to ignoring them or, at the very least, putting them into perspective.

They say that a picture is worth a thousand words. Here is an example straight out of my own very unpredictable daily life:

Craig's To Do List:

1) Just Do It
2) Have No Excuses
3) Focus on What Matters
4) Perform Random Acts of Kindness
5) Rock the Boat
6) Think Before You React (a tough one)
7) Focus on Community
8) Get Home in Time for My Kids' Soccer Games
9) Stay Open to the Ideas of Others

Craig's Don't Do List:

1) Don't Worry About Things You Have No Control Over
2) Don't Wait Too Long to Act
3) Don't Discount Other People's Feelings
4) Don't Shut Out Salesmen (another tough one)
5) Don't Believe In Limits
6) Don't Be Pushy
7) Don't Forget: Family First
8) Don't Ever Stop Believing in Yourself

Simple. Just fill in the blanks. We've all heard the propaganda about writing things down, and it's true. Writing it down makes your list tangible. It increases the likelihood that you'll follow through.

We all have the power to decide. We can decide where and on what we want to focus our energy. We can recognize those issues over which we have control and those we can influence. We have the power to decide whether or not to take action. We have the power to make leadership a verb.

Moving Forward

Huntington's Disco and Dining was a source of pride for me even if it wasn't as off-the-charts successful as F.U.B.A.R. I had made my fair share of mistakes, but the mistakes weren't wasted; I learned from them. I was beginning to understand myself as a businessman, not just an entrepreneur. My priorities were changing. The property management company was new and exciting. It was requiring more and more of my time and energy. I knew the club was going to suffer if I didn't make a change. This was something I could control, something inside my "circle of influence."

And then there was Deborah.

She and I had met back in my F.U.B.A.R. days. Deborah wasn't a big clubber, but she did come in once in a while, and she knew I owned the place. Deborah was flat out beautiful. She's just as lovely today. What she saw in me remains somewhat of a mystery even today.

Here's the story. Back in those days, I shared a house with two of the bouncers who worked at F.U.B.A.R. Donnie and Mike were cousins, each a bona fide Adonis: tall, handsome workout fanatics. The girls loved them.

The three of us shopped at a Smith's Food King in the neighborhood. Deborah worked there as a checker while she was going to school. Any guy with a brain in his head went to Deborah's line.

One day, Donnie goes in, buys a six-pack of Coke and a bag of chips, and walks through Deborah's line. These were the days before the bar-code scanner. Checkers used what they called "the 10-key-pad." So here's Deborah doing her 10-key-pad thing and drooling over this 6'3" blond hunk. Donnie heads for the door, and Deborah calls to one of the box boys, "Go find out what kind of car he drives."

The box boy hurries out and returns a couple of minutes later. Turns out that Donnie drives a 12-year-old beater, more rust than paint, the passenger side door tied closed with a rope. Not too impressive.

A week later, in comes Mike. He fills a basket with non-essentials and heads for Deborah's line. Here's Deborah doing her 10-key-pad thing and drooling again. Mike heads for the door, and Deborah says to the same box boy, "Check out his car." Which he does.

It turns out that Mike's car is a 15-year-old Datsun that starts about half the time and looks worse than Donnie's wreck. Not too impressive. A couple of days later, yours truly makes a stop at the store for milk and cereal. I head for Deborah's line. I won't say that she's exactly drooling in this case – at 5'10" and 140 pounds soaking wet, I wasn't the Adonis kind – but I'd like to say I could hold my own.

Same line to the same box boy: "Get out there and check out his car."

I may have only been 5'10" and 140 pounds, but I drove a Porsche Targa in those days. That was all Deborah needed to know. For the next six months, she swooped down on me like there was no tomorrow. True story.

It's also worth mentioning, I think, that, above and beyond my really hot car, Deborah and I hit it off famously. Lots of laughter, lots of good times, lots of positive energy. Lightning in a bottle for six months, and then she was accepted into a special marketing program at the University of Southern California. Just like that, she moved on. I moved on. I even got married for a short time; a complete failure.

Fast forward three years. After Deborah graduated from USC with a degree in Food Management, she called me. She wanted to know if my dad might be able to help her find a job since he'd spent 30 years in the food industry. This may not have been the question I was hoping she would ask, but I called my dad nonetheless. With his help, Deborah was able to land a job in San Diego. Less than a year later, good fortune brought her back to Ventura when a position opened up with Nabisco.

She and I hooked up again, and the chemistry was even stronger than before. Except for one small problem. These days I was driving a five-year-old Chevy Nova, the disco was on the market for the third time, and I had just started Huntington Property Management.

Some people may have seen a guy on the skids, but not Deborah. I asked her to marry me, and she said yes. When her boss at Nabisco said, "What in the hell are you marrying this loser for?" she answered, "He had it once, and he'll have it again. He'll have it again, because he likes it."

So with Huntington Property Management now managing two condominium complexes, I put all my eggs in that basket.

I had no intention of being in the nightclub business and trying to find success in a marriage. I wanted to be home at the end of the day. I wanted a family. *Focus and priorities.*

I also wanted a successful business, and I knew there was serious potential in the property management field. Success in my eyes meant pushing the envelope, running my own show, and making good money.

Deborah was right. I liked it then, and I like it now.

The Art and Science of Persistence

Former basketball great and U.S. Senator Bill Bradley liked to say, "Ambition is the path to success. Persistence is the vehicle you arrive in."

I like the fact that he doesn't hesitate to weave ambition and persistence into the same picture. We've been talking all along about how leadership is a verb meaning to "take action." Think about how much taking action is impacted by ambition. Some people view ambition as a dirty word, as if it is somehow tied to greed and avarice. That's not how I see it at all. Ambition, in my view, is wanting to achieve, to rise above circumstance and put your stamp on something. Ambition is a good thing. It drives us to succeed, just like Bill Bradley was saying.

Persistence, as he notes, is very much the engine that makes almost anything we strive to achieve possible. Persistence is a mindset. It's not one of those things that one person has and another doesn't. This isn't musical talent or great athleticism we're talking about here.

––––––

Persistence is getting up in the morning and vowing to make something happen; and if you come up short, going after it again and again until the job is done.

––––––

Huntington's Dining and Disco had not been an extraordinary financial success, but it did prove to be an exercise in persistence; I can look back and be proud of that. It's also worth mentioning that the process of selling the disco was a lesson in persistence all its own.

It took me three tries to sell the club. The first two guys who put the club under contract failed miserably, mainly because they were trying to improve upon my business model. In both cases, I was forced to repossess the club for non-payment, which was the very last thing I wanted to do in either case. However, the third buyer was a Hispanic gentleman who packaged the club for a Hispanic audience, Oxnard's primary population. He did his homework. He understood his market and that disco was becoming increasingly popular with his audience. He understood timing. He understood the product and the culture; he brought in the biggest Hispanic bands from Mexico, and people flocked to the club.

Lessons learned:

- **Determine your audience.**
- **Know your product.**
- **Know your competition.**
- **Consider your timing.**
- **Do your homework.**

Putting the Lessons in Play

I knew one thing about the property management business, even with less than a year of experience under my belt. The industry was antiquated. Condominium complexes were clearly open to a new way of doing business, so my timing was good.

I changed the model. While most property management companies hire vendors to take care of such things as the pool and Jacuzzi, and to handle such chores as the landscaping and the common area maintenance, I changed the model around completely. I took on those contracts myself. Then I hired the necessary people and bought the necessary machinery to satisfy the contracts. It was an investment upfront, but it paid for itself immediately.

I decided to office on site, so I bought a unit in the Port Hueneme complex and converted it into an office for the association. Since I wasn't living there, the city and the county didn't raise a stink.

I instituted the lockbox idea for the Port Hueneme complex much as I had for the Cabrillo Park Condominiums. From then on, every homeowner sent his or her homeowner's fee directly to the bank. The bank opened every envelope and deposited every check directly into the association's interest-bearing account.

This gave me more time for soliciting new business. Condominium complex #3 came into the fold three months after going into the business fulltime. Casa San Carlos was a 100-unit complex with a terrible track record for maintenance and a dissatisfied homeowners association. The Casa San Carlos board heard my pitch. They liked my hands-on approach. They liked the inclusive way I approached the management of Cabrillo Park and Port Hueneme, and after I talked to several board members at both complexes, they hired Huntington Property Management to handle their affairs.

Know Your Strengths

I'm a big picture guy. I like acting on a vision. I like getting the ball rolling. I like getting my hands dirty.

I am not a detail guy. I don't like crunching numbers. I don't like sitting in an office. But I knew very soon after signing our contract with Casa San Carlos that I needed someone who liked the details, enjoyed accounting, and didn't mind holing up in our office.

I had met Bob Collins at Cabrillo Park. He was on the association's board of directors. He was also the controller at the Santa Barbara Biltmore. Bob was exactly the kind of guy I needed, and he was ripe for a change. In his business, companies like the Biltmore transfer their employees every three or four years, almost like clockwork, and Bob and his family were tired of moving. So I made him an offer of 30% of the stock in my business, and he became the controller for Huntington Property Management.

We made a good team. He handled the office and all the accounting. I spent most of my time pitching our services. Over time, we would grow to 63 complexes and thousands of units. We made decent money. Did we get rich? No. Back then, the property management business was not a get-rich business. It was too cutthroat; it lacked industry controls. In fact, there were no industry controls and no licensing. All you had to do was print a business card and go knocking on doors. All homeowner association contracts were 30-day-contracts. If we bid $6.00 per door, for example, the next guy could come along and tell the homeowners association, "Well, we'll manage your property for $4.00 a door."

Back then it seemed that every board of directors had one gadfly, usually a retiree who thought the best way to do his or her job was to cut costs, even if it meant a cut in services (which it always did.) At every board meeting that one member always took over and turned it into a bitch session. And the person they bitched at was the property manager. A homeowner didn't come to a meeting if he didn't have a complaint; the two went hand in hand.

I would walk into a board meeting, lay my hands on the table, and think, "Okay. I'm here. Drive the nails in."

Conducting business at a board meeting was difficult in particular because every homeowner thinks of his or her building as his or her castle. Understandable, but not always conducive to decision-making or common sense. Good thing I had a sense of humor.

One of my favorite stories – the kind that made me want to pull my hair out, but was far too common – concerned the president of the board of a 100-unit complex. This was another of those complexes where our firm did everything, including the landscaping. The president was a lady long on Social Security with little else in her life except her sacred association duties. She insisted I put the empty fertilizer bags on her front porch so she could be absolutely certain we weren't over-charging her. It was crazy, because the association wasn't paying me for the fertilizer; they were writing a check directly to the supplier.

Another guy accused me of taking kickbacks from the chemical company who supplied the chlorine for his complex's swimming pools. This association used about 300 gallons of chlorine a year. The guy had called the chemical company and was told the price was $1.60 per gallon. "Your invoice said it was $1.65 a gallon. You're getting a kickback."

"What are you talking about?" I said calmly.

"I called them. You can't deny it."

"Well, I'd better call them too, because they charged me $1.65," I said. I figured it out. A nickel per gallon kickback would have paid me all of $15.00.

This was the typical mentality of the association's most vocal board member. This was the guy who lost the third grade election for hall monitor and has been stewing about it ever since. There are four other great members on this same board, people who really do have the best interest of their association in mind, but this guy makes life miserable for everyone.

As strange as it sounds, there are always certain advantages to working under less than ideal conditions. You just have to dig them out and make the most of them.

In our case, all of our contracts were 30-daycontracts. A 30-day-contract kept you hungry. I was always selling, and I love to sell. Bringing a new complex into the fold was always a rush for me.

However, 20 years of dealing with 30-daycontracts and board members whose agendas were not always good for the association was a pretty good run.

I had learned as much about relationships as I had the intricacies of a niche industry that most people take for granted. I had created or enhanced a number of tools that were, in many respects, unique to the industry. I had taken an aggressive approach to packaging services that benefited my clients and also provided my company with more opportunities. I had tweaked the lockbox system to such a degree that it was an ideal banking tool for me, and one that I saw as having far-reaching potential.

This was a crossroads. We all face them. I was ready for a change. I was ready for a new challenge. Was I willing to make the leap? There is security in the status quo, but I was not very comfortable with the status quo.

I also had a new goal. I wanted to get into the banking business.

Chapter 6

Think Better Habit

Two Plus Two = Five

What does this mean? It means we get trapped in our thinking. What happened yesterday will surely happen again tomorrow. What was true yesterday will surely be true tomorrow.

This is hardly the "thinkingoutofthebox" mentality we've been discussing. For every idea we conceive or for every strategy we implement, the odds of that idea and/or strategy living on as the best we can do is silly. We can always do better. We can always "build a better mousetrap," as the saying goes.

I set out to build a better mousetrap.

The first step was to emancipate myself from Huntington Property Management, and I made it clear to Bob Collins, my longtime partner, that I was ready for a change. Bob was not a personality guy; he would sit in his "cave," as we called his office, and do his 10-key-pad thing all day long. He agreed to buy me out, but first he needed someone like me to be the face of the business. So we recruited a personality guy. The three of us came to an agreement, and I was free to start anew.

———

Starting anew meant taking something I had learned
early on in my days as a property manager
and putting it to good use.

———

When I first contracted with Cabrillo Park to manage their 80 units, we were using ledger cards to bill the homeowners for their monthly fee. The system was ripe for misuse, and even abuse. Everyone from the board to the guy in the one-room condo thinks the property management company is stealing his money, not surprising since they were writing their checks to the company and mailing them off to some unknown address that could have been anywhere. My first thought was: This is silly. No wonder no one trusts anyone.

I changed the model.

My idea at the time was simple on the surface, but really somewhat revolutionary in creating a new way of thinking, an example of what I call the "think better habit." There always has to be a better way.

So I thought, "How can I do this?" And the answer was this: "When I mail out the statement for the homeowners association fee, the address on the return envelope will be the bank's address, not my office or my post office box."

This simple change proved to alter the homeowners' perceptions. Now they were thinking, "My money's safe now, since I'm not sending it to that corruptible property manager, who I just know is stealing us blind."

The idea saved me time, since I was no longer opening a stack of envelopes, endorsing them, and then traipsing over to the bank to make a deposit. But saving me time and money was not my primary goal. Doing this allowed me to go to the boards of the complexes I was managing and say, "Here's how it works now. Your money goes directly into the bank. To get the money out, you and only you sign the checks."

Now I am no longer touching their money, and no one can accuse me of tampering with their funds. It was a simple matter of trust that made it easier for a complex's board members to consider switching their management contract to me.

Every day, the bank would send us a list of the homeowners who had paid that day, and we would enter that information into our accounting system. Simple.

As I mentioned, I began this lockbox concept with a small branch bank in Oxnard called Hacienda Federal Savings and Loan. In exchange for their willingness to process all my homeowners' checks, I deposited $40,000 into an account at their bank. This was 1979, the era of the savings and loan debacle, and Hacienda was flying high. They were also the first bank to fail when the crisis came full circle three years later and people started going to jail. Fortunately, the government took over Hacienda and all their deposits, so we came away unscathed. I moved our operation over to another local bank called Santa Paula Savings and Loan, one of the few to survive the crisis. By then, however, Huntington Property Management was running nearly a dozen complexes, and had deposits of just over a million dollars. We were quick to see the advantages of the computer in our daily operations.

Most property management firms back then ran on a shoestring. Cutting corners was a way of life. I decided early on that presenting a more efficient, updated management style – the kind that actually saved the clients money without cutting back service would pay immediate dividends. It did. Every upgrade made it easier to woo homeowners associations. They even began seeking us out.

One Step Ahead of the Game

Larry Pothast and Mike Kennedy walked into my office on a cool spring day in April of 1984. Larry and Mike worked for the Bank of San Francisco in the marketing and finance departments. The appointment had been on my calendar for two weeks; they wanted to introduce us to a new program the bank was using. Okay, fine. I was always willing to listen. I believe that managers are too quick to dismiss the input and ideas of other people. In fact, keeping an open mind to new ideas can't be overestimated. How many times have you hung up on a salesman or said "Take me off your call list," even before you've heard what they have to say.

I have a rule of thumb: if a salesman has the guts to call me, I always do him the courtesy of listening. If he or she leaves a message, I call back. I never know what I might hear. And Larry and Mike were the perfect example. Had I not invited them into my office that day, my career path may have gone in a completely different direction.

We shook hands, and I invited them to sit. I offered them coffee.

"Thanks for having us," Larry said after stirring cream and sugar into his coffee. "We have a new banking program that we've developed that we'd like to talk to you about."

"Homeowners associations love it," Mike assured me.

"Anything that makes them happy makes me happy," I said.

"We called it 'lockbox,'" Larry explained, excitement oozing from his pores. "Payments from the homeowners are sent directly to us instead of to you. We open the envelopes so you don't have to. Then we deposit the money, and send you a statement."

"Simplest thing in the world," Mike said.

I nodded. "Yeah, I do that already. Works great."

Their jaws dropped. Mike managed to say, "What? What are you doing already?"

I said, "My checks get mailed directly to Santa Paulo Savings and Loan. They open the checks and deposit them right into our account. Then they send me a list of all the people who have paid, and we enter the information into our computer."

"Oh," Larry said. He was down, but not out. He sat up in his chair. "So how are you entering your information into the computer? Are you doing it by hand?"

"How else?" I wanted to say. But I didn't. Larry had my interest. So I replied, "Yeah. By hand. Why?"

"Because we have an easier way."

"If you work with us, we send you a disk everyday with all of your information on it, and all of your data entry," Mike explained. "Then you slip the disk into your computer, hit 'load,' and zip, the information loads all by itself."

"All in about two minutes," Larry added.

"So every day you're going to send me this disk. How are you going to do that from San Francisco?" I asked dubiously, but also with considerable interest. Remember, this was 1983. Al Gore hadn't invented the Internet quite yet, and everyone was still using 5 ½ inch floppy disks. So it wasn't that dumb of a question.

"We'll send it by courier. Hand delivered. We do it all the time," Larry said. "As soon as the checks from your homeowners have been entered into our system and deposited into your account, we'll have a guy headed to your office with your disk."

Now my head's spinning: Just think, no more data entry, no more data entry clerk working four hours a day punching numbers into the computer. Now those four hours could be used on marketing and sales. I looked from Mike to Larry and asked the obvious question, feeling pretty confident I knew the answer. "And what are you going to charge me for that?"

"Oh, we're going to do it for free. All we want is your business, Mr. Huntington," Mike replied.

———

I got up from my chair. I walked around the desk to my office door. I closed the door. I turned around and stood there with my arms folded over my chest. Mike and Larry looked at me as if an inmate had just escaped the asylum. I said, "You're not leaving this room until we sign a contract."

———

Just like that. I didn't have to think about it. I knew I was going to save time. I knew I was going to save money. It was a no-brainer.

It was also the start of a very fruitful business relationship. The following week, I transferred all my banking interests involving

Huntington Property Management to the Bank of San Francisco. They provided a lockbox account for all of our complexes and delivered their data entry disks every day, like clockwork.

In came the era of the computer, and we were quick to see the advantages. We switched from punch cards and paper receipts to electronic information sharing with our bank. It was still all about who had paid and who hadn't, but now the turnaround was far faster. And, we were working far smarter.

As computer systems evolved, their methods evolved and so did ours.

Above and beyond a solid business relationship, two fine friendships also grew out of that fateful day. Mike, Larry, and I hit it off from the very beginning. We socialized on a regular basis. Every time they came down to Ventura, we grabbed our clubs and played a round of golf. After golf, they would often come up to my house to have dinner with my family. Larry even taught my son, Craig Lee, how to perform all sorts of magic tricks. One night after dinner, Larry started playing the piano to the total fascination of my other son, Matt. I believe Matt's appreciation of music started that night.

Every time we got together, I'd look at them and say, "This is really the life. When I grow up, I want to be a banker."

It was a running joke. But the truth was, I wasn't kidding.

Chapter 7

Focus on Communication

Address the Problem; Solve the Problem

It sounds ridiculously simple, doesn't it? You have to address the problem to solve the problem.

The genesis of the problem isn't really the issue.

The problem can be work-related. You're having issues with your boss, your colleague, your staff. You're running into problems with your product line, your supplier, your distributor. Sales are off. Morale is down. People are under-performing.

The problem could be personal. You can't get a date. You're overweight. You can't get yourself to the gym. You can't seem to find that job or hobby that really moves you.

The problem could stem from a relationship. Your significant other doesn't communicate. Your kids are hanging out with the wrong kind of people. Your friends don't seem to call as much.

We all have our own list.

The key always has been and always will be effective, open communication. Being both open and effective is not as easy as it sounds. Why? Because most of us fail miserably at consciously "focusing" on communication. We take it for granted. I talk, you talk. What's the big deal?

Some guy named George Bernard Shaw summed it up this way: "The problem with communication ... is the *illusion* that it has been accomplished."

Communication is both verbal and non-verbal, so it's more than just the words that come out of our mouths. It's also about our intent and our sincerity. Too often what we think is communication is just trying to get our own way, to win a point, to make an impression.

And then there is the truly perplexing problem known as "active listening." Most everything we learn is through listening, and most of us aren't very good at it. On average, they say that we only remember about 25% of what we hear. Why? Here are five common blunders that impair our ability to listen, retain, and learn:

- **We forget to Acknowledge.**
- **We forget to Probe.**
- **We forget to Be Quiet.**
- **We forget to Leave Out the Emotion.**
- **We forget to Ask for Clarification.**

We're always trying to figure out how to get our own points across instead. We're always figuring out what we're going to say next. How can you probe or acknowledge or ask for clarification if you're already thinking about the next thing coming out of your mouth?

Going for the Gusto

I was ready for a change. I had been in the property management business for 20 years. I had been successful, insofar as that business would allow. I had made good money, if not great money, and worked my fingers to the bone. I didn't mind working my fingers to the bone; on the contrary, success and hard work go hand-in-hand nine times out of 10.

———

I wanted to be a banker. This was both my goal and my problem. I wanted to bring my expertise in the property management world and apply it to the banking world.

———

I wanted to be the guy who went out into the world of property management groups and sold them on the idea of using my bank to funnel their homeowners' fees. I wanted to create a lockbox concept that made their lives so easy that they would have no reason not to deposit every nickel from their various condominium complexes into my bank.

I didn't wake up one morning to the sudden revelation of Craig Huntington, banker extraordinaire. I had been nurturing the dream for some time. I had kicked it around with Larry and Mike, my friends from the Bank of San Francisco, for years. I had talked about it with my wife Deborah numerous times.

It's not that jumping off the bridge of change is, necessarily, more difficult the later in life you get. I don't believe that. But this was different than opening a rock 'n roll nightclub at the age of 22, when I had little enough to lose and no one in particular to explain my actions to other than my investor. And this was different than selling off F.U.B.A.R. and jumping into the disco scene with Huntington Dining and Disco, with little or no knowledge of that very trendy scene.

Now I had a family. I had a wife who was raised in the San Fernando Valley. She was a valley girl through and through. She had matriculated at UC Santa Barbara, UC San Diego, and the University of Southern California. She had never lived farther than 10 miles from the beach her entire life. Same with my kids. Our house sat on a hill in Ventura with a view as spectacular as any in Ventura County, three stories with glass on three sides and fruit trees crowding the hills, assuring us every ounce of privacy we could ever ask for.

———

Unfortunately, my dream for going into the banking business would require my family to uproot from California, and move to some as yet undetermined location where the lockbox concept had not taken hold.

———

Larry and Mike had offered me a position in a bank they had just acquired in Texas. I considered it. Mike and Larry had become great friends of Deborah and me, and their offer was not only fair, but damn generous. But there was a problem. Personality wise, Larry and I are like two peas in a pod. He is gregarious and outgoing. He's a dynamic public speaker. He walks into a room and everyone knows him. Ninety percent of the people love him; the other 10% can't stand the guy. Same with me. Larry goes into a bank and makes a huge splash. He makes a presentation at a property management seminar, and the lights go on. I'm another Larry in many ways, and Mike, a banker's banker who shows up in a suit every day and plays by all the rules, knew this. We both did. It was like, "Damn, if I go to work for them, I'm just another Larry, only one more rung down the ladder."

I didn't want that; nor did Larry and Mike. They wanted the best for me, and I wanted them to be as successful as possible. I was grateful for their offer. But in the end, I think we all understood that it was best if I declined.

And more than that, this was one of those watershed moments when you realize that risk is, in fact, a road worth traveling. I did my research. I studied the markets. I saw the exploding growth in and around Las Vegas and decided this was the place to launch my new career: Craig Huntington, Banker.

Now if I could just convince Deborah, my personal valley girl, that I wasn't completely crazy. I chose the direct route. Here we were in beautiful Southern California, a city on the water, the boat harbor, the islands, the house on the hill, and I come home and say, "We're moving to Las Vegas. Pack your bags, honey."

I have to give Deborah credit. She didn't go off the deep end. She didn't threaten to divorce me. She didn't threaten my life. She heard me out. She knew I hadn't been particularly happy after 20 years of managing 60 or 70 condominium complexes. She knew the fun had gone out of it. I would also like to believe that she had enough faith in me and my latest hairbrained scheme to see just how successful it could be.

She didn't immediately pack her bags. No use going to Las Vegas if I couldn't sell someone on my idea. So that's what I set out to do.

Communication is a Two Way Street

Cliché? Sure, we've all heard it before, but it is so obvious that we often just pooh-pooh it. In the business world, managers are often the worst at this. They often think that every word they say to their staff or their employees will be heard, understood, and immediately acted upon just because they are the ones in charge, and that's exactly the kind of reaction the boss deserves. Unfortunately, that's exactly the kind of attitude that leads employees and staff to resist, defy, and even ignore. A defensive employee is not a happy, productive employee. But an employee who feels his or her input is respected, who feels a sense of ownership in the company or a specific project, who feels empowered, not emasculated, is an employee who will go the extra mile to see a job well done.

———

Let me emphasize: this two-way communication thing is not just reserved for the workplace. It's just as important, if not more so, on the home front, in your personal relationships with friends and family, with your spouse and your kids, with everyone who's important to you.

———

This goes back to our lessons on verbal and non-verbal communication and the art of active listening.

With Deborah's and my decision to sell Huntington Property Management and to pursue a new venture at the age of 48, it was just as important for me to "validate" her concerns as it was for her to "acknowledge" my need to take a risk. It was just as important for her to "ask for clarification" about what the heck I was up to as it was for me to stop and "be quiet" so that she could effectively have her say. "Leaving the emotion" out of it was not as easy as it sounds; it never is in these kinds of situations. I wanted to respect her fears and her trepidation. I wanted her to acknowledge my excitement. This may have been my dream and my decision, but it was our lives.

The problem we all face is that it is so easy for us to lose our *focus on communication.*

I freely admit that I have a problem with this concept of communication as a two-way street. I struggle with it. I am more of a "just do it" type of guy. Listening is not my strong suit. I've learned over the years just how important active listening can be, but it still proves to be difficult. Here's what I try to remind myself:

1) **My ideas can benefit from the input of people I respect; why not take advantage of that.**

2) **Listening is a great way for me to learn; the more I know, the better I can do my job.**

3) **Listening empowers everyone around me; it's a great team builder.**

4) **Listening shows you care; it's a great relationship builder.**

Send. Receive. It sounds simple. And it is simple if you're willing to give as much credence to the receiving part of that equation as you are the sending part. That is the hard part.

Hit the Ground Running

I was confident and excited. I understood the risks. I had just sold a solid business and was venturing into a world that was far more cautious and conservative than I was, a world that was also highly regulated and not given to "thinking out of the box." This was, however, also a world that thought in terms of making a reasonable profit while offering quality services: this fit me to a T.

With that in mind, I set out for Las Vegas and started knocking on the doors of every bank in town. My pitch was very straightforward.

"So this is what I'm proposing, Mr. Banker. I want to start a new division in your bank, a division that I will head. This division will target the business of property management groups. I will offer them complete lockbox services, which include a secure system of receiving and processing of all homeowner association fees. In exchange for these services, the property management companies will agree to bank with us. In other words, I will be bringing in a steady stream of low-cost deposits. Deposits that won't cost the bank a lot of money in interest payments. Deposits that the bank can then turn around and loan out for far more interest."

**This was a new concept for the banks,
and they just were not sure how to embrace it.**

I had been self-employed with my relatively small businesses since I was 23, and had never worked in a corporate atmosphere. Many times I had asked myself how corporate managers could be so successful and yet be so totally unable to look outside their comfort zone for new ideas. It seemed to me a no-brainer. The more deposits one had, the more loans one could make, and the more money you would make.

Finally, the Business Bank of Las Vegas showed a serious interest.

The Business Bank of Las Vegas was what they call a De Novo bank, one that has been in operation less than five years. De Novo banks face considerably more scrutiny from regulators, and their failure rate is much higher than established banks.

That being said, the bank's head honcho still saw the potential of my lockbox system and said, "Let's do it, Craig."

He made it sound easy. It wasn't. I took a 70% cut in salary from what I had been making back in California. Growing my salary was contingent upon the amount of deposits I brought into the bank. For every million dollars in new deposits, I would receive a salary bump of $1,000. This meant I was in total control of how much money I made. I could live with that.

Deborah wasn't quite so thrilled. My salary was suddenly $36,000 a year. She almost had a heart attack. I told her about the upside, and she told me to start selling. No problem. That's what I did; that's what I was good at. And besides, I had a product that every property management company worth their salt would understand and want: a product with essentially no downside. The product would save them time, money, and an endless stream of headaches.

Here were the keys to my banking program and, therefore, the keys to my sales pitch:

The property management company had to save time and money; the lockbox system that I intended to install at Business Bank of Las Vegas would do both, collecting and depositing all homeowners' fees and providing the management company with daily accounting records.

The homeowners associations that the property managers represented had to make a competitive return on their money; back then, low-interest deposits accrued an average return of 3%, and I could easily guarantee this.

All that I'd ask in return was a commitment on the part of the property management company to start banking with us.

Time to get to work.

A Personal Marketing Philosophy

For better or worse, this crazy world of ours revolves around sales. It's undeniable. You can have the finest product on the planet and the most unique and innovative concept ever conceived, you can use the best materials and target the largest audience, but if you can't get your message out in an effective way, you won't be in business for long.

———

I call my approach to marketing and sales "touching the customer." In my world, there is no substitute for face-to-face contact. Shake people's hands, look them in the eye, convey a sense of trust. In other words, "touch" people.

———

It might be tempting to say that this approach is most effective in a service industry such as banking, but I would argue that it works in any business where a trusting working relationship is in order. It certainly worked for me when I was trying to woo the homeowners association of a condominium complex to trust their business to my property management company. And it would be my primary marketing device now that I was in the banking business.

No matter what your marketing or sales philosophy is, however, first you have to define your target audience with respect to your product: Sales and Marketing 101. If you're selling the best cheeseburgers in town, your marketing options range from billboards to sandwich boards. If you're promoting a concert, your options range from the Internet to window posters.

My audience for the 20 years I owned Huntington Property Services had been small and well defined: condominium complexes and gated communities primarily. Radio and television ads didn't work. Mailers were the very first things people threw into the trash.

The property management business was a people business. Homeowners associations met in crowded clubhouses or stuffy meeting rooms. Their boards often gathered around someone's kitchen table. This was a very minute, very personal group. These people were protecting something even more precious than a business entity; they were protecting their homes. I had to be aware of that.

I learned early on that my most effective tool was my ability to connect with people on a personal level. It's my passion. I'm genuine, and that seems to come across when I'm talking with people. I'm believable, one, because it's in my nature, and two, because I know that the truth is a helluva lot easier to sell than a lie.

———

My point is that everyone has to figure out his or her own style. What works for me might not work for you. What works for you may very well go against every grain of conventional wisdom. It doesn't matter. Find it. Go with it.

———

My goal was to "touch" people, and I knew I had to do it on a genuine, believable level. There was no other way. I found this out the very first time I stood up in front of a homeowners association, and tried to convince them that my property management company could manage their homes and their money better than anyone else. Shake their hands, look them in the eyes, convey a sense of trust.

When I moved to the banking side of the industry in Las Vegas, my clients were guys just like me and companies exactly like Huntington Property Services. I was, in essence, selling to men and women just like me, all property managers, all dealing with homeowners who met in crowded clubhouses and stuffy meeting halls and board members who did their business over coffee in someone's kitchen.

In Nevada, my new home far, far away from the beaches of California, there were 60 property management companies. Sixty. That was my audience. I had to sway one or two or 10 of them to do business with me and the Business Bank of Las Vegas.

I started calling on them one by one, laying out my program and trying to convince them that I had a new way of doing business that would benefit them and the associations they serviced.

Sales is a process. It begins with an introduction. But the real selling is in the cultivation of a relationship.

You can't ask a property management company responsible for up to 370 properties and thousands of units, with 10, 20, or 50 million dollars in deposits, to change horses from a bank they may have been doing business with for years to your bank as a spur of the moment decision.

You walk a fine line between pesky salesman and a provider of professional services. You walk a fine line between a guy who's making a nuisance of himself and a guy who can help make their business better, more efficient, and more profitable. I couldn't show up at a company's office every two weeks asking them if they'd made a decision on my proposal. But I still needed to be proactive, and I still needed them to know that I was there for them.

Behold, the Candy Man

The idea was a simple one. Maybe even a silly one.

After making my introductory calls on property management companies all over Nevada, I devised a plan for getting in the door a second time without coming across like a pest. I went to the local Five and Dime in Las Vegas and bought a case of glass candy jars. Then I filled them up with lollipops, Tootsie Rolls, Snickers, and BabyRuths. I taped my business card inside the jar and set out on my rounds again. Only this time my only purpose was to deliver a candy jar to the receptionist at the front desk of the 60 companies on my list.

"This is for you. If you run out, call me," I'd say to her, even though I never intended to let the jar run out.

Simple, and a little silly? Could be, but it was an approach that fit my style. I'm a guy who loves an entrance, who loves to make conversation, and who's completely comfortable blending small talk with business.

The receptionist in most offices is the gatekeeper. She (or he) is the very last person you want to tick off or alienate. If you can't get past her, you won't go far. But it was more than that, of course. The candy jar was a conversation starter.

"Where did that come from?" was the first question everyone in the office asked.

"From that really nice guy, Craig Huntington. The banker," she'd reply, or something along those lines.

Every two or three weeks I'd come by and fill up those candy jars. It was a reason to drop in. I was no longer a pesky sales guy. Now I was the candy man.

After a few months, I could walk into pretty much any office on my list, fill up my candy jar, and tour the office with a new offering. I wasn't intruding. I wasn't making a sales pitch. I was adding a spark to their day. Mixing business with my visits was part of the natural progression of integrating myself with both the decision-makers of the management company and their employees. That was just good business. And I did it using a marketing vehicle that fit my style.

———

If you're uncomfortable with the sales approach you're using, you're doomed for failure. Find what works for you – not what works for someone else – and you'll see the deals start to materialize.

———

It did for me. The contracts started coming in.

Over the years, as my sales staff grew, I always offered this piece of advice: "You've got it made when you can walk past the receptionist, march right into their offices, and use the restroom without asking anyone."

No salesperson on earth can simply waltz into a place and expect people to give him their business. You have to build a relationship first. Then, you can start "asking" for their business.

The candy jar approach is a legacy I passed on to my sales staff over the years, and to this day we have jars filled with suckers and Tootsie Rolls in management companies all over the country. Now they have our logo on them, but really nothing else has changed. Those candy jars represent my genuine appreciation for the relationships we have been allowed to cultivate over the years. It works.

110 Degrees in the Shade

Sales, of course, is all about persistence. If you can't take rejection, then you should find another line of work. And if you don't value persistence, then the entrepreneurial world probably isn't for you.

This is a story I always like to tell. I had been a banker for some years and had extended my client list into Phoenix when I took persistence to a new level. I had been calling on a property management giant called Rossmar Graham for two years. They were one of the largest companies in the area. They had deposits upward of $50 million, and I wanted those deposits in my bank. At the time, they were with Bank One and not particularly enamored with their services. I still couldn't get them to pull the trigger and make the move to us, but I refused to give up.

It was 110 degrees in the shade one day and miserable. Everyone was suffering from the heat. So before making my monthly stop at Rossmar Graham's company headquarters, I headed for the local Costco and bought a box of 50 ice cream bars.

I walked into their offices a few minutes later with the box under my arm and started shouting, "Ice cream! The ice cream guy is here! Come and get your ice cream and beat the heat!"

Heads popped up from every cubicle, and I could hear people saying, "Who is this crazy banker?"

Of course, they all recognized me by this time, and everyone came running, even Rossmar Graham's president, Jim Hanley. It was a huge hit. Also a memorable one, and not something that anybody at Bank One would have ever considered.

The point is this: I had been calling on the company for two years, and yet they could see that I still viewed them as an important viable prospect, enough so that I would go out of my way for their people. "Touching people." We talked about that earlier.

Three months later, Rossmar Graham made the switch and started banking with me. It was a $50 million coup, and worth two years of my time.

In the end, it's all about putting the "focus on communication," as we said in the beginning of the chapter. That's how problems are solved. And that's how relationships are built.

Chapter 8

In the Name of Choice

Success by Any Other Definition

Things took off with Business Bank of Las Vegas.

My first contract was with one of the bank's current customers, a property management company called Terra West. I set them up with a lockbox system, and they immediately began reaping the benefits. It was a good test model for me, and it also gave me something I could point to when I was trying to woo new customers. "Here, look how much my system has benefited Terra West and their stable of homeowners associations."

———

People like to chase other people's success. People like to jump on the bandwagon. Always give them the opportunity.

———

My second contract and the first new business I signed up was a company called Taylor Property Management. The company was owned by a wonderful woman named Pat Taylor, someone I immediately identified with because her company was not that different in size and assets than my own Huntington Property Management had been.

Pat had never heard of a lockbox system. When I asked her about her current banking arrangement, she admitted that her company banked with nine different banks around town. All week long, her company would collect and open checks from homeowners at the various condominium complexes and gated communities that they managed. The checks would accumulate from Monday to Friday while her bookkeeper prepared a week's worth of deposits. On Friday, Pat's receptionist would pack up their deposits and drive from bank to bank. The man-hours were exorbitant. So was the turmoil the system created.

So I said to Pat, "Listen, why don't you come and bank with me, and we'll take care of all of that. You won't have to collect the checks; your homeowners will send them directly to us. You won't have to open a thousand envelopes and keep track of a thousand different transactions; the lockbox system will take care of that for you. And you won't have to drive all over town making deposits. We'll do it all. And every day we'll send you an accounting that you just upload to your computer. Think of the time and money you'll save."

Pat got it. She was the first company to jump on our bandwagon.

Others followed. In nine months, I successfully swayed five property management groups to abandon their current banking situations and to begin banking with us. I set each of them up with our extensive lockbox services, which effectively relieved them of the burdensome and time-consuming task of collecting individual checks from the homeowners in their various associations. This allowed them to concentrate on taking care of their properties and chasing new business. I paid a fair rate of interest on the money deposited in our bank by their homeowners associations. I was filling the coffers of my bank with nearly $20 million dollars in deposits just begging to be loaned out at hefty interest rates.

And by all rights, I should have been reaping the benefits myself. My deal with the bank was very straightforward. For every million I brought in, I was supposed to get a thousand-dollar bump in my salary. It wasn't happening.

I was supposed to be making $58,000 per year by this stage in the game, but my raise hadn't come through.

This, naturally, led to a "minor" confrontation with the guy who had hired me, the bank's top dog.

"We have a deal," I told him. Not a handshake deal, but a signed, sealed, and delivered deal. "I bring in deposits, my salary goes up. I've brought in nearly $20 million, and I'm still making peanuts. What's going on? Where's my $20,000 raise? And what's going to happen when I bring in an additional $50 million?"

"Well, we can't pay you that much," he said.

I said, "Didn't you want me to be successful?"

"We didn't think you'd be this successful," he admitted.

I had been self-employed my whole life, and I couldn't understand the concept of a deal with strings attached. But that day I learned that I really knew very little about banking. That was also the day I really began to learn about the business.

Know What You Don't Know

Banking, I discovered that day, is all about ratios. As important as any ratio in the industry is "deposits to loans."

Banks don't make money on their deposits; in fact, they pay interest on most deposits. They make money by loaning out those deposits at whatever rates of interest the markets will bear. The ratio is extraordinarily significant. If a bank is paying an average rate of interest on their deposits of, say, 3% (which is about what it was back in 1999), and they are loaning out that money at 8%, then they're reaping a fairly significant profit. But if they have more deposits on hand than they can lend and are unable to attract sufficient customers, the money sits in a vault at the Fed, and the Fed pays them 2%. Now the bank is losing money.

If they're not making loans, then the deposits don't mean a thing; actually, the deposits generate a loss. My job was to bring in deposits, and I was having success at that. Their end of the deal was making loans, and it wasn't happening.

I could have blamed the bank, and I could have blamed the man who hired me. But I didn't. It was my fault. I should have been better versed in the industry.

In the case of the Business Bank of Las Vegas, they were loaning out only 60 cents on every dollar they had in deposits. They sure didn't need any more deposits, which meant they didn't need me. At the very least, they weren't going to pay me for bringing in deposits they couldn't loan. It was an ugly situation.

A Watershed Moment

Someone once said, "Limits exist only in your mind."

Someone else once said, "Know your limits, but never accept them."

I like to think of myself as an advocate of the first guy's school of thought, but I also understand where the second guy was coming from. Here's what I do when I give a presentation or a speech to people in my industry, or to classrooms filled with ambivalent students, and the subject of creating viable, meaningful habits comes up. I go to the blackboard or to my PowerPoint and spell out four very simple, very straightforward rules of thumb that I've used for more years than I care to remember:

- **Take action. Now!**
- **You have NO excuses.**
- **Don't believe in limits.**
- **Think before you react.**

Naturally, all four are tied together, and one is no more or less important than the others.

Taking action doesn't necessarily come naturally to all of us. It always did to me. I have always been impulsive. I have always loved being in the middle of the fray. I've always been addicted to results.

Not everyone is like that, and maybe that's a good thing. For some people, taking that first step is the hardest part of the process. This can lead to a lot of inaction and a lot of regrets.

For me, whether it was going out on the campus of Oregon State in Corvallis and registering more first-time voters than any other campus in the state, or jumping into the car at a moment's notice and driving 500 miles to some place I'd never been before, I rarely ever waited for someone else to take the first step.

Whether it was opening a rock 'n roll club at the age of 22 with no money and no experience or jumping into the disco business because I thought it was time for a change, I never looked for a reason why I shouldn't do something. I only looked for the reasons why I should.

When trading in my nightclub interest for the chance to start my own property management company – a lack of experience be damned – I always believed in my capacity to work harder than anyone else and my willingness to face the unknown.

With the desire at age 45 to sell the company I had built for 20 years and jump head first into the world of bankers and bank regulations, I always found risk a road worth traveling.

––––––

Taking action has never been my problem. Nor has the issue of making excuses. I rarely make excuses, even when the obstacles seem more or less insurmountable, probably because I'm too stubborn to take no for an answer.

––––––

The issue of limits is another matter. Overstating your limits is just as debilitating as thinking you have none. Every man and every woman has limits, but when you start focusing on them, you're as good as beaten. That's what I mean when I say: don't believe in limits.

My biggest problems often stem from reacting before I really think something through. That's my impulsive side, for better or worse. Here I was in Las Vegas, nine months into a new venture, and the bank I was working for was refusing to pay me. I was doing too good a job.

I had a decision to make. Was I really cut out for banking? In many respects, these fine people didn't think like me. They were bound and shackled by rules and regulations that government agencies were imposing on them. Here was this very small bank, by most standards, and you had to requisition everything, even paper clips. There were no spur of the moment decisions. There was no improvisation. I could only imagine what a huge institution like Citibank or Bank of America was like. Compared to my property management business or my nightclubs, the banking industry was confined by a lot of outside forces, and I had to decide if I could prosper in such an environment.

I didn't think too long about it.

I knew I wasn't going to work for a guy whose word meant nothing. He was the kind of guy who told me that my assistant couldn't attend the company Christmas party because he was a temp (even though he'd been working for me for nearly a year.) He was the kind of guy who viewed his staff with such contempt that he once said to me, "Don't worry about staff, Craig. Staff is like a desk. If it doesn't work out, just get a new one."

No, I couldn't work for a guy like that.

However, I also knew I wasn't ready to give up on an idea I knew was viable. I still wanted to be a banker. I just didn't want to be a banker with Business Bank of Las Vegas. I knew there had to be people in the banking industry who had the same philosophy that I did, and similar values. I just needed to find them.

So I quit. I handed in my resignation to the bank. I left without another concrete prospect in hand, but confident I could find another bank that would see what I had accomplished in less than a year at Business Bank of Las Vegas.

This was an opportunity. There was no other way to look at it.

Choices

I like the guy who said, "When you have a problem, make a choice... you'll feel better." The guy's name is Dr. Shad Helmstetter. He's a behavioral psychologist, who also was wise enough to add, "Choosing to live your life by your own choice is the greatest freedom you will ever have."

Choice is about controlling who you are and where you're headed. Making the decision to leave Business Bank of Las Vegas would not be the last time I would face such a crossroads; in fact, 10 years later, I would walk away from a $500,000 a year position for similar ethical and personal reasons.

Too often we're controlled by outside forces that suggest we should do one thing because society tells us to, or we do another because so many people have expectations for our behavior. The trouble is, society isn't guaranteeing your happiness. Neither are your friends or your family, no matter how well meaning.

———

Inviting happiness into your life is not a job you can subcontract or outsource. It's up to you and only you. And the best tool you have in your arsenal when it comes to being happy is your ability to make choices.

———

In my case, I had a family to think about. They had supported me by coming to Las Vegas. They had given up their lives in California and believed in me enough to back my decision to pursue a new career. A year into the game, and here I am essentially starting over again.

And now I had a new adversary: the Voice of Treason.

The Voice of Treason

Who is this guy? The "Voice of Treason" is that voice in your head saying, "Buddy, you're no good." We've all heard it. We all have those negative vibes trying to drag us down. It's human nature.

Whenever I speak in public on such subjects as communication or leadership or strategic planning, I'll ask my audience to raise their hands if they've ever heard that voice in their heads that's telling them, "You can't do it," or "You'll screw it up if you try," or "You're going to fall flat on your face and look silly, so forget it." Most everyone knows what I'm talking about, and almost everyone raises his or her hand. For those who don't, I say, "You know that voice in your head that's insisting you don't raise your hand"…That's the voice I'm talking about."

We all have the voice.

Here's something to remember. The Voice of Treason doesn't play fair; the Voice of Treason plays upon your fears, and there's not a person alive without some fears. Fear is an instinct. It's a good thing when it comes to our survival, but not such a good thing when you're trying to follow a dream or take a risk. Our biggest challenge is often distinguishing between fear and feeling, fear and fact, fear and reality.

Kicking the Voice of Treason's butt is a continuous process. We have to do battle with that negative voice almost every day. It's part of life. Get up, put on the gloves, and give the Voice of Treason a left hook even before you turn on the coffee.

And the good news is, the more often you put the Voice of Treason in his or her place, the less often the voice jumps up to bite you.

I had to deal with my Voice of Treason after resigning my position at the Business Bank of Las Vegas. The voice was absolutely working overtime. "Hey, buddy, you're no good."

I didn't listen. The truth is, I've never been very accommodating to my Voice of Treason. The best antidote, I've always found, is taking action: getting back on the horse, hitting the pavement. That's exactly what I did back in December of 1999.

Don't Just Decide: Do

You know how often this scenario plays itself out: You make a decision, and the decision gets lost along the way. Maybe you're waiting for someone else to get things going. Maybe more "urgent" matters take precedence. Maybe ambivalence leads to inaction. Maybe fear leads to paralysis.

In any case, it's essential to realize that deciding is NOT doing. There is a step in between. It's like walking to the edge of the bridge with every intention of jumping, metaphorically speaking, and then standing there looking down at the water. That doesn't count. You have to put the decision to work. You have to take the leap.

Don't just decide: go out and do it.

Take the action necessary to see a decision through, knowing mistakes are probably inevitable, knowing you might trip and fall, knowing you might fail miserably, knowing you might have to start over. But also having enough faith in your decision to know that success might very well be right around the next corner.

Chapter 9

Jumping Off the Log

No Such Thing as a Sure Thing

I have always gotten a kick out of an oft-repeated quote attributed to former Chicago Bears quarterback Jim McMahon, when asked about taking risks. He said, "Yeah, risk-taking is inherently failure-prone. Otherwise, it would be called sure-thing taking."

I'm not sure if Jim had his chosen profession in mind when he said this, but the truth is, his insight fits the business world as well as it does the world of sports, and it's remarkably apropos when it comes to our personal lives as well. To trade a football analogy for a baseball one: You can't get a hit if you're not willing to step up to the plate and swing away.

There are no guarantees that the new business you're thinking of starting will be a success, but there is absolutely no chance it will be a success if you're not willing to travel down that road and put yourself at risk.

There are no guarantees that the girl standing at the end of the bar will turn out to be the girl of your dreams, but you'll never know if you don't walk over there and say hello.

There are no guarantees that you'll be able to lose that 10 pounds you've been dying to shed, but you'll never know if you don't commit to that new diet and new exercise programs.

It's like we said in the last chapter: Don't just decide – Do it.

———

Forget the "sure things" in life. Creating something special takes guts. It takes courage, pluck, and a willingness to fall flat on your face.

———

You've heard the saying: If it was easy, everyone would be doing it. To me, that's good news. After all, who wants to travel down the same path as everyone else?

Politically Incorrect

We live in a society where everything has to be just so. It seems that fewer and fewer of us are willing to say or do what we really think for fear of sounding insensitive or politically incorrect. It's a dangerous precedent. Differing opinions and conflicting points of view are the things that made this country great. Freedom of speech and freedom of action are at the heart of the Constitution. Rocking the boat is not something to be avoided on the offhand chance that we might just hurt someone's feelings.

It seems sometimes that we worry about everything: How something we say is going to be perceived. How something we do might go against the grain. How failing might look bad in someone else's eyes.

I grew up riding a bike without a helmet, and if I choose to ride a bike without a helmet today, it's no one's business but my own. If I want to jump in the back of a pickup truck and cruise Main Street, that's my decision. I'm not hurting anyone else.

———

I say rock the boat, if your heart tells you to. I say go against the grain, if it helps you follow your dreams or brings you a sense of joy. I say fail now and again, knowing you can get back up and try again.

———

We've become a country that no longer demands that people contribute to society. It's okay if a kid drops out of high school or has a child out of wedlock. It's okay if we're becoming less and less literate compared to the rest of the world. It's okay if there are more violent crimes in this country per capita than almost any other country in the world, just as long as we're politically correct and don't hurt anyone's feelings.

The truth is, it's not okay, and most Americans are sick of being politically correct.

The truth is, most Americans see a growing segment of our population leeching off society, producing little, and expecting more.

There's nothing wrong with the expectation that everyone carry his or her own weight. There's nothing wrong with encouraging people, young and old, to get off their butts and make something happen. It's not politically incorrect to expect people to contribute to society if they're able.

Fear and entitlement go hand in hand. Sometimes we're afraid to jump off that log into the unfamiliar. Sometimes it's just easier to sit back and expect everyone else to do the heavy lifting.

The problem is, too many dreams go right out the window if you let fear and entitlement get control of things. And we're so much more likely to contribute to society and to build a legacy for ourselves if we chase those dreams and take those risks.

A Second New Beginning

The year was 1999, and I wasn't the only guy to leave the Business Bank of Las Vegas right around that same time. My friend and colleague Bob Skertich had been in the bank's sales and marketing department, and also had an issue with the way the bank was managed. Bob had since hooked on with First National Bank of Nevada, which was owned by a savvy entrepreneur named Raymond Lamb.

The sequence of events proved important. A year earlier, Ray had started a De Novo bank called the First National Bank of Arizona. As I mentioned earlier, De Novo banks are essentially start-ups. The regulations are stifling and the chances of going under are sky high. Ray was doing it anyway.

Several months after starting First National Bank of Arizona, Ray purchased the Laughlin National Bank. Laughlin is a town of 10,000 right on the Arizona border. Ray renamed this new enterprise the First National Bank of Nevada.

Since my departure from the Business Bank of Las Vegas, I had been pounding the pavement in Reno, Henderson, and Las Vegas, approaching banks with my lockbox system and cultivating relationships that I hoped would result in a situation similar to the one I had just left, only with a bank that was actually dedicated to making new loans. There was interest in the concept, but no one was ready to make the commitment just yet.

That's when Bob Skertich called, and I will be forever grateful that he did.

We talked earlier in the book about the value and absolute necessity of cultivating positive relationships, in the workplace, at home, and in the community. As we said, nothing in the world can replace a respectful, trusting relationship, and that's what Bob and I had developed during my time at Business Bank of Nevada. I liked how he approached his job, and he could see how I approached mine.

"Craig, you've got to meet these guys," Bob said when he got me on the phone. He was talking about his new employers at First National Bank of Nevada. "You'll love what they're trying to do, and I'd bet anything that their number one guy will jump at your lockbox idea."

"Let's do it," I said. "Can you set me up a meeting?"

Bob did set up a meeting, and it would turn out to be the most important of my career. A week later, I was in my car driving to Scottsdale,

Arizona and meeting with Ray Lamb, sole stockholder in the First National Bank of Arizona and the First National Bank of Nevada.

———

I liked Ray right from the start. He had grown up in rural North Dakota. His first job was picking rocks out of a local farmer's wheat fields. His second job was a jack-of-all-trades at a small, family-owned bank appropriately called Lamb's Bank.

———

Ray studied law at the University of North Dakota and opened a law office in his hometown. He made his first splash in the banking business when he was 29, and went out and acquired a share in a small local bank. Along the way, he found his passion. By 1992, he'd built a mini-empire of banks that stretched from North Dakota into Minnesota, and he sold the lot of them to US Bancorp because he saw the potential in one of the country's fastest growing areas: Phoenix.

"I got lucky, Craig," he told me of his next venture in 1992. "I bought the Bank of Arizona at just the right time. Things got crazy, and we grew that darn bank from $13 million in assets in 1992 to $229 million by the end of 1997. I can tell you that surprised a few people."

———

Clearly, Ray Lamb wasn't lucky. He was smart and aggressive.

———

He sold the Bank of Arizona in 1997 for a pretty penny to Norwest, signed a one-year non-compete, and jumped back into the banking business when he started the First National Bank of Arizona the minute the non-compete expired.

"I want to take Arizona and Nevada by storm," he said to me.

"Good. And I think I can help you do it with the lockbox system I've developed," I replied.

"Okay. I'm interested. Give me your pitch," he said.

So I did. I started at the beginning and told him about my experience in the property management business with Huntington Property Services. I explained to him how I had developed a lockbox system long before anyone had ever heard the term, only at the time I was on the other side of the fence; I was the property manager making the deposits, and Hacienda Federal Savings and Loan was the one reaping the rewards. "Then I sold my company and came to Las Vegas. I started a lockbox program with the Business Bank of Las Vegas. I brought in nearly $20 million in deposits before it became clear that they didn't have the wherewithal to make enough loans to cover the deposits."

"And now you'd like to do the same for my bank, is that right?" Ray replied.

"Exactly," I said.

Ray shrugged. "Ah, hell, we're already losing money. What's one more salary."

He laughed when he said this. So did I. "What's one more salary" wasn't exactly a roaring endorsement, but what the heck; I was back in business.

And I would come to find out that this was Ray's style. He knew people, and he trusted his instincts. I had described a business model that made sense to him. He knew the idea could profit his business, and he liked the guy who was selling him the idea. We shook hands. He said, "So let's talk numbers, Craig. How does a $40,000 salary and four basis points a month sound?"

In banking terms, 100 basis points equals 1%. So four basis points equalled 4/100 of a percent. It doesn't sound like much, does it? But think of it this way. For every million dollars in deposits I brought into Ray's bank, he was going to pay me a bonus of $400. So if I made my goal of bringing in $20 million in deposits, I would be making $8,000 a month, or $96,000 a year. Not bad. And if I some how managed to bring in, say, $100 million in deposits, I would be making $40,000 per month, or $360,000 a year. That's good money for a sales guy with a bulletproof plan.

For the moment, I was guaranteed a salary of $40,000 a year. It was a cushion. Time to get to work.

First National Bank of Nevada

So the Homeowners Association Division, or HOA Division, of First National Bank of Nevada was created. This gave my new operation an official air. Property management companies who chose to bank with us would be dealing with a separate entity, a division created just for them and their special needs. I was given the title of Vice President of First National Bank of Nevada. Of course, in the beginning, it was just me. I had no salespeople. I had no staff, and wouldn't need one until we landed an account and started my lockbox system.

I set up an office with "HOA Division" stenciled on the door and my nameplate alongside. I was in business.

All well and good, except for one small challenge. I still had to reckon with staff and personnel completely unfamiliar with the property management business or the world of homeowners associations. The men and women inside First National Bank of Nevada and Arizona lived in a world of policies and procedures that served, essentially, as their bible. Banking regulations were like the Ten Commandments, only they were written on unbreakable stone. Don't even think to question them, because as sure as the sun will rise tomorrow, the next set of auditors will be in the office next month making sure none of the rules and regulations have been in any way tampered with. Staff and personnel had no other choice.

Unfortunately, I wasn't cut from the same cloth. Yes, I was a banker, but I still had an entrepreneur's spirit.

Recognizing that I possess more of a property manager mentality in my approach to the business than I do a banker's point of view has always proved to be a good thing, because I understand my customers.

My customers are property management companies and the men and women who own them. I was once one of them, and I knew that managing condominium complexes and gated communities, where your clients are homeowners associations run by occasionally fickle, unpredictable, and demanding boards of directors, was unlike managing most other types of businesses. There is a personal nature to the business that is hard to replicate elsewhere. Why? Because the product in question is the home (or homes) that people live in. The product is their castle. Property managers get this; I was a banker now, but I still had a property manager's role in my repertoire.

The HOA Division of FNBN was my own creation, by and large; Ray Lamb gave me that latitude. The products I was selling – in particular my lockbox procedures, banking solutions that saved my customers time and money, and my personalized management style – were my own creation as well. But I couldn't aggressively and successfully sell the products, and do so with complete confidence, if I didn't have a partner who gave me the responsibility and the authority to make it fly. I had that now. I had Ray Lamb and his First National Bank of Nevada and Arizona.

The future looked bright.

Don't Just Talk the Talk; Walk the Walk

This idea of talking the talk while failing to walk the walk is one that is certainly prevalent in the business world, but it is rampant in government. And I admit it. I find myself increasingly frustrated with the men and women we elect to run our country. We are no longer problem solvers. We don't tackle the issues of the day. We are no longer committed to finding answers.

I get tired of hearing long-winded speeches weighed down by generalities that essentially mean nothing. I think most Americans do. I honestly don't give a damn about speeches and posturing. Go do something. Tackle a problem. Be willing to fail. Be willing to make a mistake. Quit worrying about your next re-election campaign and become the public servants you were elected to be.

Politics in this day and age is all about staying in power, dragging the other guy down, and protecting your backside. The concerns of the men, women, and children of our nation, and those of future generations, are way down the list of priorities of our so-called elected officials. There is very little long term problem-solving because what happens in the future can't positively affect a politician's re-election campaign. And there is little short term problem-solving because you might offend the special interest groups paying for those re-election campaigns.

**I want to stand up and shout: Go do something!
Go solve a problem.**

I'm a conservative on most political issues, as are most bankers, but I am considerably more liberal when it comes to business. I don't believe in having a lot of meetings and discussing strategy. I would rather set a strategy and execute whatever tactics it takes to see the strategy implemented.

I have discovered, however, that a good number of people in corporate America feel very strongly about meetings. In fact, they have one meeting after another, but are generally in no hurry to convert whatever it is they are discussing into action. They may kick around a strategy, but they are not the best at implementing the tactics necessary to see the strategy through.

Most of what goes on in the banking industry is determined by government banking regulations: This is what you can do, and this is what you can't. It doesn't leave a lot of room for entrepreneurship.

Ray Lamb was different. Ray was more entrepreneur than company man. He believed in hiring aggressive, creative people, in particular when it came to sales and marketing.

My first few weeks on the job at FNBN were dedicated to building my lockbox system. I had to set up operations, programs, and processes within the First National Bank system, create appropriate accounts dedicated to my potential customers, even come up with a signature card that made it easy for homeowners associations to access their accounts.

These rather elementary steps – elementary by my way of thinking – required any number of meetings with any number of people inside the bank: financial guys, compliance people, computer programmers, operations people, attorneys. Problem number one: I have always been accustomed to being the boss. "We need this done. Please do it. Thank you very much."

What I found instead was a sequence of meetings where we covered the same ground over and over again. I began to ask myself why it was so hard to approve something as basic as a signature card. I began to look around the room and realized no one was even taking notes. Apparently we hadn't had enough meetings, and that, after all, was often the case when change strikes a heavy chord in many businesses: "Let's have another meeting just to be sure."

––––––

Too many people refuse to jump off the log and make decisions. Decisions suggest a level of responsibility, and who wants to be responsible in case something goes wrong?

––––––

So by the fourth or fifth meeting, I decided to take the bull by the horns even though I'd only been onboard for a month or so. I began taking notes. The idea was to hold people accountable for what they were saying and doing, or not doing, as was too often the case. I began creating what are now known as my infamous "To Do Lists."

A "To Do List" is essentially a mission. Give people a mission, give them the tools to complete the mission, and show your faith in their abilities, and they'll almost always go that extra mile for you.

I would never say, "Charlie, I need that signature card by Friday." I would say, "Charlie, we need that signature card. When can you get it for me?"

Now I've given Charlie ownership. He's invested. Now he knows he's part of a larger goal, that of getting the HOA Division off the ground. Now he's willing to jump off the log. Now he's willing and able to create his own momentum and actually get something done.

Strategies and goals are great, but there is always that watershed moment when everything hinges on a headlong plunge into action. You can't navigate the river if you don't jump off the log.

Chapter 10

And Your Purpose Is?

Why This?

We all have to be able to define our goals. We have to be able to say, "This is why I'm doing exactly what I'm doing."

We have to be able to answer that question for every person in our organizations. We have to be able to say, "This is where we're headed and why."

If you can't clearly and concisely state what your purpose is, you'll have one heck of a time getting out of bed every morning with any kind of zest and gusto. You have to be able to answer the "Why this?" question. Why this job? Why this relationship? Why the choice?

A wise man named Thomas á Kempis, a fifteenth century author and monk, once said, "Every day we ought to review our purpose, saying to ourselves, 'This day let me make a sound beginning.'"

I have to believe that á Kempis was referring to the bigger picture of the lives we lead, but I also think he was acknowledging that purpose comes in smaller doses too. Knowing why we're doing what we're doing should be a question we ask with regard to things like our mental and physical health, what we eat, the way we parent, the way we choose our friends, the direction of our careers. Knowing our purpose – or the answer to the "Why this" question – gives us incentive to act. It serves to drive us. It can motivate us. It's that thing that lets us make a sound beginning every morning.

15

Creating a Mission Statement

A mission statement is something every organization is supposed to have that gives meaning to its existence and a foundation to its underlying purpose, that reinforce the values that caused the organization to come into being, and that underscores its vision.

Mission statements in the business world run the gamut.

I always liked Coca Cola's: *Everything we do is inspired by our enduring mission to Refresh the World… in body, mind, and spirit; to Inspire Moments of Optimism… through our brands and our actions; to Create Value and Make a Difference… everywhere we engage."*

The people at Google kept theirs short and sweet: *Google's mission is to organize the world's information and make it universally accessible and useful.*

The HOA Division's mission statement went like this: *Our mission is to provide the highest quality niche banking and unparalleled customer service for property management companies and homeowners associations nationwide.*

A mission statement is not supposed to be a bunch of esoteric words written with the sole purpose of impressing investors or wooing customers. It's supposed to be that one statement that keeps a company and its workers grounded and, hopefully, gives them purpose.

I'm also a strong believer in the personal mission statement. I say why not have a written statement that actually spells out what you're trying to achieve as a human being, something that provides the backdrop for your purpose and puts some spring in your step.

This is my personal mission statement. It captures the items that are important in my life and ensure my focus. It outlines the big rocks that I put in the jar first and spells out the structure that I build the rest of my life around:

- **Be the best father and husband I can be.**

- **Create and grow a good place to work that has great financial returns.**

- **Perform random acts of kindness.**

- **Live to serve my talents as a communicator, artist, and independent businessman.**

- **Create balance in work, play, and community.**

- **Inspire those I interact with.**

A mission statement, whether it is personal or professional, has far more impact if it is written down and made accessible every day. I feel that impact just looking at my own mission statements written here on this page. My advice? Put your written mission statement in your wallet or purse, tape it to the mirror in your bathroom, or tuck it in the corner of a picture frame on your desk at the office. The place is not as important as is the likelihood that you'll see it once or twice a day, and be reminded of the words you've created to describe your mission.

Committing your mission to writing makes it more concrete. The actual words staring back at you does several things: it inspires you to act because you've dared to bring your mission to light; it increases your commitment to the success of your mission; it heightens the pride you feel in something real and important.

Putting it to Work

We said it earlier. The HOA Division's mission was to provide the highest quality niche banking and unparalleled customer service for property management companies and homeowners associations nationwide.

In real terms, that meant there were three things that defined our purpose when it came to sales and marketing.

First, when I walked into the offices of a property management company – whether they managed 1,000 units or 100,000 units – I needed to show the people in charge that changing to our bank would save them time and money, enough time and money that it would significantly affect their bottom line. This is the old adage about always appealing to the pocketbook. And while this is true, I also needed to prove to the management company that our lockbox system would come with personalized attention to their needs and the best possible customer service.

At the same time, I had to provide the homeowners associations that the property management companies represented with a "win." And that "win" was a sufficient and competitive rate of interest on their money. Remember, the deposits that the property management companies were putting into our bank did not belong to them; the money belonged to the homeowners association. The boards of directors representing these various homeowners associations needed to see that their money was earning enough interest to keep them happy. And because we had a division dedicated exclusively to property management companies, our overhead was small. This allowed us to offer just slightly higher interest rates than everyone else. This was a huge advantage.

And lastly, the HOA Division – my division – had to convince the property management company to bank with us. That's where it all began. In other words, we had to get their deposits.

———

So there were three entities that needed to come away from any deal I struck feeling as if they were better off than before I walked through the door: the property management company, the homeowners association, and my bank.

———

We made the property management company money by saving them time and man-hours.

We made the homeowners association money by providing them the best possible interest on their deposits.

We made my bank money by giving them the resources to go out and make loans.

Herding Cats

For the first six months of my tenure with First National Bank of Nevada and Arizona, I was rarely in my office. I was a one-manwrecking crew. I was on the run 10 to 12 hours a day. I was visiting property management companies in two states. I was cultivating relationships with their employees, leaving overflowing candy jars at offices from Phoenix to Las Vegas, and spreading the word about my lockbox.

That's how the art of sales works. One of my father's favorite sayings was: "You don't make any money sitting on your ass behind a desk."

In the first few months of my employment with Ray Lamb's First National Bank group, I reported to a gentleman named Dave Groshon. "Reported to" might be a slight misrepresentation, but Dave did sign my expense report. I always figured that the guy who signed my expense report was, in fact, the guy I reported to. Dave, in return, sent reviews of my progress to Ray Lamb, even though Ray and I met on a regular basis anyway.

One day, Dave inadvertently left a copy of his three-month review on my desk, and I couldn't resist taking a look. It wasn't a particularly flattering review, and one line stuck out from all the others.

"Keeping track of Craig is like herding cats," was how Dave put it.

Herding cats? Was he kidding? This, obviously, was neither a good evaluation nor a complimentary one. The truth was, it stung. I could only imagine how Ray may have viewed such a comment, but I wasn't exactly in a position to defend myself since I had gotten the information from a confidential memo.

Instead, I took some time to consider what Dave's comment meant and realized, in the end, that he really had no clue what I was doing. He may have understood, to a degree, what I was trying to do in terms of bringing in new customers to the bank, but he certainly didn't understand what was involved in getting the job done.

———

Dave didn't realize that I couldn't do my job from behind a desk, the way many people do. It didn't work that way.

———

Dave didn't realize how much time went into cultivating relationships with the people in the property management companies I was targeting; these men and women operated on a face-to-face basis just like I did.

Dave didn't realize how much time I needed to spend on the road or how many hours I needed to spend sitting down with prospective clients, talking with them, getting to know them, gaining their trust.

Sales, at this level, is a face-to-face business. It's a patient business. You can't touch someone sitting behind your desk. And even with all the road time and all the face-to-face time, things didn't happen overnight. People didn't move five, or 10, or 20 million dollars in deposits from one bank to another on a whim. It took time building bridges and selling a concept like the lockbox. I was nine months into the job before I delivered $10 million in deposits to the bank.

If You Don't Trust in Your Ability, No One Else Will

It doesn't matter what profession you choose, what game you play, or what goals you've set for yourself: if you don't believe you've got what it takes to deliver the goods, no one else is going to believe it either.

After reading Dave's less-than-flattering review of my performance, I made a decision. I had to trust in my ability to make the HOA Division a success. I planned to keep doing what I was doing. I also decided I should keep Dave better informed of my comings and goings and the progress I was making. This was not easy for me. I have never done well answering to people, but I have always recognized the need for open and straightforward communication. In any case, it is always better to have an ally in your camp than a detractor. It just makes life easier.

If Dave knew how much I trusted in my own ability to build the HOA Division into a vital cog in the bank's overall success, he might actually start trusting me enough to let me do my job and stop, as he put it, herding cats. And if I did my job well enough, he might even benefit.

Suddenly, things started to pop. Suddenly, all the relationship-building I'd been doing began to bear fruit. With each new account I brought into the bank, I added credence to my program that I could then use as demonstrative proof in enticing other property management groups to jump aboard.

———

My goal was to make a property manager's decision to switch to our bank a no-brainer; a win-win that no one else in the industry could match. It started to pay off in a big time way, and we were drawing in new customers almost faster than we could keep track of.

———

I couldn't have done it without Ray. He was an anomaly among bankers. He embraced innovation. He supported new product ideas. He rewarded out-of-the-box thinking.

In other words, he and I had graduated from the same school of thought. We made a good team, and we were both destined to prosper from the relationship.

The Fast Track

By 2002, the First National Banks of Nevada and Arizona were growing by leaps and bounds. The company topped $1 billion in assets that year. This was remarkable, almost unprecedented growth given the fact that the First National Bank of Nevada started with the purchase of a small $70 million dollar bank in Laughlin. The media credited this astounding growth to a booming southwestern economy, which was true, but they didn't give enough credit to the personal service and niche marketing we were doing.

———

The HOA Division by this time had literally exploded. We hit a milestone in May of 2002: $50 million in deposits. This was $50 million that the bank now had at its disposal for the purposes of making loans at very lucrative interest rates.

———

Enter the subprime lending phenomenon.

Chapter 11

Your Best Asset is You

Decade of Irresponsibility

It's pretty simple. A subprime loan is a loan that is made at a higher interest rate than most other loans. The great irony behind this is that these are loans made to borrowers who do not qualify for ordinary loans because they've either racked up a poor credit history, don't have a salary that can realistically support such a loan, or are at risk for some other reason.

It goes without saying that there is a much higher risk of default on these so-called subprime loans.

The subprime market really began to gain traction in the mid-1990s. It was during this time that Wall Street and the government both started to endorse the whole concept. "Everyone should be able to own a home," was how the politicians framed it. So banks started to jump in with a fury. With Fanny Mae and Fanny Mac guaranteeing these loans, the number of participating banks tripled by 1997 and tripled again by the time our bank jumped into the fray. With high profile politicians like Barney Frank and Christopher Dodd demanding that bankers make these loans so that "everyone can own their own house," who could blame them? They saw this as a risk-free road to solid earnings.

But of course there was a risk. We've seen the fallout. It was irresponsible to lend money to buyers who were not qualified to pay those loans back. And there is plenty of blame to go around, from the buyers and the lenders, to the government agencies who pushed the programs, to the Wall Street firms who were so eager to participate.

———

The question for our purposes is this: when is risk NOT a road worth traveling? And the answer is when and if the government becomes the driving force guiding your actions.

———

In the subprime fiasco, we had buyers who were blind to the possibilities of a housing crisis. We had lenders selling the notion that housing prices would never go down. We had government agencies making claims they couldn't possibly meet and politicians spouting dangerous and non-sustainable rhetoric about "homeownership." We had Wall Street financial firms pushing the envelope of illegality, and doing so knowingly.

Whom Do You Trust?

We've all heard the three most commonly spoken lies of all time:

1. The check is in the mail.
2. You can't get pregnant the first time.
3. It's not you. It's me.

Or more recently:

1. My dog ate my homework.
2. What happened between me and that other woman was meaningless.
3. No, you don't look fat in that.

My favorite lie of all time is the one every politician on the planet has spoken or inferred since the beginning of time:

"We're the government, and we're here to help you."

Surely some politician proclaimed the exact same sentiment – or something very close – when subprime mortgages were touted as the best thing since sliced bread. "I'm here to help you."

———

No, the government is not here to help you. In fact, when the road you are about to travel down is in some way tied to trusting the government, the risk is not worth it.

———

First and foremost you have to trust your own instincts. When that voice inside your head says, "Go for it," then you probably should. And when that same voice says, "Forget it," you'd better listen.

We all make mistakes. We all fall flat sometimes. But it's far easier to get back on the horse if the only person you can blame is yourself. It's the same with success. Follow your instincts. When things go well, you can pat yourself on the back and say, "Well done."

During the subprime fiasco, most people's instincts were telling them that the flaws were too obvious. This can't work. You don't lend money to people without the means to pay the loan back. Not everyone should be a homeowner, despite what the politicians were saying.

So what happened? Greed took over. People were trusting bureaucracies and institutions without a leg to stand on. The results haven't been pretty, to say the least.

Sustainability - *Not*

There is a huge difference between taking a healthy risk in pursuit of something worthwhile and viable – like your goals and your dreams – and chasing an unhealthy risk based purely on making a fast buck.

Back in 2002 and 2003, Arizona and Nevada were hot enough real estate areas without the subprime market; with it, business flat-out boomed.

For our bank, the business was coming so fast that it was hard to maintain our asset-to-capital ratio.

Ray never took a penny out of the business. He paid himself a
salary of $500 per month. Everything else he dumped back
into capital, which allowed the bank to grow unimpeded.

A huge chunk of the bank's loans went to developers speculating on
the housing boom. A good percentage of the rest went to subprime
mortgages. Those were our niches, for better or worse.

A year later, the bank counted its customers on both the personal
and business side of things at 19,000. By the end of 2003, assets had
topped $1.7 billion.

In just seven months, from May of 2002 through January of 2003,
we doubled our deposits and reached another milestone: $100 million
in deposits. I was making a very healthy six-figure salary. Ray was living
up to his end of our working arrangement. He had a personal credo:
"You make money for me, you make money."

Had Ray expected me to do so well? He may have been a little
surprised, but he never said so. In me, Ray saw a guy who worked at a
different pace than most. I was all in, 24 hours a day, 7 days a week. I
ate, drank, and slept the work scene. Even when I was at home or on
vacation, the wheels were always turning. I'm in my early 60s now, and
nothing has changed. That's just the way I'm built.

So to say that Ray was thrilled with the division's progress and its
contribution to the growth of his bank was an understatement.

Your Best Asset

If you're an entrepreneur or a young executive, and you want to
identify your best asset, just look in the mirror. You are your own best
asset. Your talents, your knowledge, and your attitude are three things
you can and must control.

There were really two primary reasons why I was successful. The first will sound a bit arrogant. It may sound as if I'm bragging, and I don't want it to come off like that. But the first reason I was successful was the guy staring back at me in the mirror every morning. I had developed a product extremely well-suited for my clientele, and I was able to do that because I had once walked in their shoes. I knew the market and understood their needs. And I was able to convey that in a personal, hands-on sort of way. I was my own best asset.

Being your own best asset is one part knowing what you're good at and one part knowing what you're not good at. Maximize what you're good at and find someone to help with the things you aren't.

The second reason I was so successful in establishing the HOA Division was Ray's willingness to loosen the reins and let me run with the program. Few banks will do that. Most are slaves to their compliance departments. Ray's view of this was simple: If we're abiding by the regulations, then make it work. If a policy is inhibiting growth, then change the policy. If something is preventing us from serving our clients to the best of our ability, then fix whatever that something is.

Going Nationwide

I had been with the firm 2 ½ years when I got a call from the head office, informing me that Phil Lamb was starting to work at the bank and I would now be answering to him.

Really? Okay, so who in the hell is Phil Lamb? Obviously, he was kin to the owner, but I'd never met anyone by that name. I did some research. Turns out that Phil was Ray's 28-year-old son. My first thought was that this can't be a good thing, not a good thing at all. Someone with my independent bent and absolute need for autonomy answering to the boss's son; I couldn't see it working. The very first thing I did was to flout my resume out on the marketplace. I even sat down for a couple of preliminary interviews with two other banks.

Then I met Phil. It turned out that he was one of the smartest guys I was ever likely to meet. He had graduated at the top of his class at Georgetown, passed the CPA exam with flying colors, and went on to graduate Summa Cum Laude from Harvard Law. He spent a few years working as an investment consultant in Boston, before deciding to join forces with his dad.

Phil and I hit it off. There was good chemistry right from the beginning.

Right off the bat, he said, "I'm going to sign your expense reports, but you're going to continue to run the division. The caveat is we're going to have to renegotiate your contract. At the rate you're going, we'll be paying you a couple of million a month, and we can't afford that."

I had been expecting this. The 4-basis-points a month was not realistic given the growth we were generating. I was willing to sit down and talk it through.

———

I have learned one thing. You have to be reasonable in your pursuits. You have to look at things from both sides of the fence. You have to look at the big picture. And you never cut off your nose to spite your face.

———

I had owned my own businesses my entire life. I understood the bottom line. I understood that a company needs to be profitable if its employees are to be well compensated.

I wanted both. I wanted my company to be highly profitable so that I could be well compensated.

So Phil and I sat down and renegotiated my deal. I came away satisfied. So did he.

This led to our next order of business. It came from a rather modest suggestion that Phil had about adding a sales representative in Colorado. I thought this was a good idea, since we had already made a formidable dent in the Arizona and Nevada markets. Then, once the ball got rolling, we began talking about a more aggressive expansion even yet.

"Let's look beyond just Colorado, why don't we? Why not look at expanding in a big time way. Let's try to get out of our own footprint. What if we hire five people?"

This was easier for Phil to suggest, since he was spending his family's money. It was slightly daunting for a local bank to consider moving into markets dominated by other, better known banks, but I could see the potential.

Remember the three rules we established in Chapter Two:

- **Have no excuses.**
- **Refuse to believe in limits.**
- **Think before you react.**

Phil's brother-in-law, as it turned out, was a headhunter, and Phil wanted to turn him loose. This was a good test of refusing to believe in limits, but it also posed the perfect opportunity to think before I reacted.

The result was this: We would search for the best five people for the job, regardless of their locations. I wasn't as concerned about where they were from, but rather how effective they could be.

I knew the markets would take care of themselves if we found the right mix of people. The response to the headhunters netted several good candidates, and we started interviewing. First, I wanted my people to know the industry ropes as well as I did; that was imperative if they were going to go out and sell our lockbox system to our select group of prospective clients. Second, I wanted them to reflect the personal "touch" approach that I used. I wasn't looking for a clone, but

I was looking for someone who would be a positive reflection of the division and all the unique features we were able to offer. Those were the keys.

There were a few other banks offering lockboxes, but we were well ahead of the curve in terms of our products, our technology, and our customer service. We could take in far more checks, and process daily deposits far faster, than any of our competitors. And we specialized. In many ways, we acted like a bank within a bank, a bank that targeted a single client base with unparalleled knowledge of the property management industry. We were in a class by ourselves.

We had the right product, and now we had a growing reputation: the HOA Division of First National Bank of Arizona was the place for property management companies to bank.

The reason I was more concerned about finding the right people as opposed to the right markets was that our sales reps didn't need offices; they just needed to understand the workings of my system, and they needed to know how to present the advantages of the system to potential clients.

———

Hire good people. Make sure they buy into your goals.
Inspire them. Motivate them. Give them the tools.
Then let them do their job. That's my motto.

———

The new sales staff began to fall into place. I found one in Houston, one in Dallas, another in Washington DC, a fourth in Minneapolis, and finally someone in Denver.

Community Association Banc

With our new sales people in place, an interesting problem surfaced. We were going national, and yet we were still called the HOA Division of the First National Bank of Nevada. That wasn't going to sell in Minneapolis, much less Dallas, Denver, or DC. We needed a new name. We needed a new identity. Something that inspired confidence worthy of a nationwide entity.

We kicked around a dozen names before I hit on Community Association Banc; banc with a "c" since we were not officially a bank. The name would read:

Community Association Banc
A Division of First National Bank of Arizona

We would de-emphasize the tagline, of course, since we wanted to portray ourselves as a stand-alone entity which, in many ways we were. I had another issue as well. I knew how homeowners associations worked. They were closely knit groups of men and women trying to protect their homes and the maintenance of their communities. They liked dealing with locals. If someone in St. Paul, Minnesota saw that the envelope for his or her assessment check was addressed to a bank in Arizona, I knew there was the potential for negative feedback. I could hear someone complaining to his or her property management company: "What happened to the homegrown bank we were dealing with before?"

The solution was easy. We would establish local post office box addresses in Dallas, Houston, Minneapolis and so on, which suggested a local presence to match our sales representative in that area. The checks would be mailed to the p.o. box, and then sent overnight delivery every day to Phoenix.

———

The bottom line is this: I would rather create a small inconvenience for myself and my staff if the trade-off is a more confident, more satisfied customer. Never give your customer an excuse to say no.

———

People look for reasons to say no. I would rather overwhelm them with reasons to say yes.

A last potential problem with our expansion plans, from my point of view, was control. No, I was not then and am not now a control freak. However, I was then and continue to be, today, a *quality* control freak.

Now the company I had created and the service I continued trying to perfect were moving into a new stage of development, and I was determined that this new stage would have my stamp on it at every turn.

I now had a staff of five fairly independent people from Dallas to Washington DC, ready to sell my lockbox system to property management groups all across the nation.

———

I didn't want to step on their toes, but I also wanted them to understand my vision. I wanted to motivate them and give them the benefit of my experience, but I also wanted each of them to feel as if he were his own best asset.

———

I just needed to figure out the best way to do that.

Chapter 12

The Power of Perception

It Begins With Experience

You may be familiar with this equation: Experience = Perception = World View.

Every experience we have shapes, augments, and expands our perception, which in turns enhances our view of the world. This is an ongoing process, but we can give it a positive boost by increasing our exposure to new experiences, new people, new places, and new challenges.

We can also make the process increasingly relevant by being open-minded, by forcing ourselves out of our comfort zones, and by realizing that we create our own boundaries the minute we think we have all the answers.

This goes nicely with a quote made famous by da Vinci, who said, "All our knowledge is the offspring of our perceptions."

This was an exciting time for me. All of a sudden, my newly-christened Community Association Banc (CAB) had taken a significant step outside the parameters I had initially developed when I sold my property management company in California and uprooted my family to Las Vegas.

We had a mandate to grow. I was a banker with an opportunity for nationwide exposure to a program initiated with a local bank. It was, in many ways, unprecedented in the industry.

We talked earlier about our action roadmap, and this was a perfect time in my career for me to revisit the five habits I so often spoke of in my leadership and communication seminars. Here they are again:

1) **Just Do It**
2) **Think Different**
3) **Communicate 'Good'**
4) **Focus on What Matters**
5) **Think Better**

Focusing on these seemingly simple steps and making them a conscious part of your day naturally creates "experience." By virtue of our decision to hire five salespeople nationwide, I had to evolve a new mode of operations. I now had to train, supervise, and assist these five people in becoming the kind of company representatives that I wanted; I was, in essence, responsible for their success, and their success (or failure) would reflect on me. Here were my three primary objectives:

- **First, make them aware of CAB's mission (in other words, make certain they bought into the goals I had set for the company).**

- **Second, give them the tools necessary for accomplishing those goals and the freedom to use them.**

- **Third, provide them with motivation above and beyond the very nice salary they could earn.**

At the same time, I had to maintain the local accounts we had already developed and that had already produced $100 million in deposits.

I was rarely in the office before, but now I was traveling out of state as well, and doing so on a weekly basis. My comfort level with public speaking now became an even greater asset, because a good number of my introductory presentations were conducted in front of audiences ranging in size from 10 people to 100.

America's Number One Fear

You guessed it: public speaking.

Even more so than death itself, people fear speaking in public. Not me. I love speaking in front of an audience, the bigger, the better. I got started back in college when I was involved in what seemed like every activity on campus. Things like running for class president and drumming up voter registration were natural venues for speaking in front of people. I thrived in that kind of environment.

When I opened my nightclubs, I loved to stand up in front of a Wednesday night crowd and emcee the various contests that clubs back in that day and age regularly featured. I was in my element even then, getting the crowd fired up and making it as fun as possible. And, of course, there was monetary reward as well. The more fun it was, the more money I made.

I attribute a considerable amount of my success in running my property management company to my ability to get up in front of homeowners groups and make a presentation that was easy from them to understand, one that empowered them, and one that made our working relationship a win-win situation.

Homeowners associations and their boards were a tough crowd. There was a fine line between getting their attention and raising their ire. There was a fine line between speaking to your audience and speaking down to your audience. This was where I learned to mix humor with content. This was where I learned to judge my audience even before I hit the stage, and to adjust my tone and style accordingly. This was where I honed my own personalized presentation style.

I also cut my teeth speaking in front of the local chapter of the Community Association Institute, an organization representing property management firms all over Southern California. I got my first break with CAI when my friend Larry Pothast had to cancel a presentation to a group in Pismo Beach back in 1988, and the President of the CIA chapter called and asked me to stand in. My topic was *The One-Hour Board Meeting.* Don't laugh. Keeping a homeowners association board meeting to one hour was an art, and nearly impossible. I'd seen board meetings run six or eight hours; that's what you get when you have a bunch of sincere and dedicated retired people with nothing else to do in one room.

I learned very quickly how to control those situations, and I imparted some of that knowledge in my speech. It went well, very well, in fact, and I found myself speaking at more and more industry functions over the coming years.

I speak off-the-cuff, even though I know exactly where I'm going with my subject matter. I never use a podium. I like to roam the stage, leaving a trail of my notes on the floor, and encouraging audience participation as often as possible. I tell stories. I use the simplest of PowerPoint presentations, and I leave hoping I've given my audience some useful tools and a positive outlook.

This is the slide I always end my talks on communication with:

Now there's a message for any situation.

Perspective

My favorite quote about perspective, from entrepreneur and businessman Allen Klein, goes something like this: "A little perspective, like a little humor, goes a long way."

My favorite story about perspective occurred back in the mid-1990s when my property management company, Huntington Property

Services, was in its heyday. I was even doing a radio show once a week; homeowners would call in and ask my advice on their various and sundry property issues.

Here's what happened. A board member for one of the homeowners associations that we represented was walking through his condominium complex one day, when he noticed that one homeowner had replaced the sliding glass doors on the back of his home with French doors. The board member went ballistic. He claimed the homeowner couldn't do such a thing without permission from the board. Turns out, the homeowner had gotten permission from the complex's architectural committee in accordance with the complex's by-laws.

The matter should have ended there, but it didn't. The board member had an ax to grind.

"I don't care who he got permission from," the board member raved to me and anyone who would listen. "He didn't get permission from the board. I want to go after the guy." This over a pair of French doors that actually looked pretty darn nice.

Letters were written. A lawyer was retained. Everyone, including me and the board's lawyer, told the board member he had no recourse. The homeowner had followed the rules. He was in the clear. The board member didn't care. He was up in arms and wanted to sue.

The guy obviously had no life other than his board membership. He was acting irrationally and refused to listen. So this is what I did: I had one of the guys who worked for me call my radio show and pretend that he had the very same problem as the homeowner who had installed the French doors.

"Now the board is threatening to sue," my guy said over the phone.

Playing my part, I said, "Now you're sure you got permission to install those new doors."

"Absolutely. From the architectural committee."

"Okay, good. So here's what you're going to do. You're going to file a counter suit against the board and this particular board member,"

I said, knowing that the board member and all his cronies listened to my radio show. "Sue the hell out of them. You'll make a fortune. The board member is being unreasonable. He has no recourse. Sue the hell out of him."

The next day I was sitting in my office, and the board member came by. He stuck his head in and informed me that he was dropping the issue. "We're just going to drop the whole matter of the French doors. It's over."

I didn't have to ask him why. I knew he wasn't dropping it because his lawyer told him he should. And he wasn't dropping it because his property management company was telling him he should. He was dropping it because he'd heard it on the radio from a guy he hardly knew.

Perspective! It's amazing who and what we allow to influence us, but the more informed we are about the power of perception and the experience it creates, the more likely we will be to choose our influences wisely.

The Business Side of Perspective

I began my career in banking with a goal of bringing in $20 million in deposits for my bank. I reached that in 18 months.

I reached the $100 million plateau in deposits after three years.

From 2002 to 2003, I saw our deposits jump by almost 175%.

Now I had a nationwide network – small though it may have been in the beginning – and I realized my perspective of the markets had changed dramatically. If we were able to grow the company by even half the amount it had grown over the last year, we could feasibly reach the $1 billion mark in deposits in seven years. I was tempted to say "no way." And I didn't want to look too far into the future, but we have been talking all along in this book about setting goals, having no limits, and being willing to go for broke. Maybe a billion in deposits wasn't a pipe dream after all.

———

I was excited. If it seemed a little overwhelming in the beginning, I reached into my bag of reliable tools and grabbed for the ones I had leaned on since before I could remember: work hard, work harder than everyone else, and enjoy the ride.

———

I created a very effective working model with my salespeople. I wanted them to be the face of Community Association Banc with their individual clients, meaning the property management companies that they were calling on day in and day out. But I also wanted to build an aura around CAB that enhanced its nationwide image and made the bank a household name among property management people everywhere.

My plan was to make myself available for speaking engagements, seminars, and presentations with industry organizations all around the country. Now that we had opened offices in five new market areas, I was also able to extend my affiliation with the various chapters of the Community Association Institution (CAI) in those areas. This created new opportunities for me to talk in front of audiences packed with potential clients.

We had a running joke back then: I would fly into town, and one of my salespeople would pick me up at the airport. They would take me to whatever speaking engagement they had arranged, and I would say, "Wind me up, put me out there, and let me do my thing."

"My thing," even on stage in front of an audience of 200, was to "touch" people. This approach can be summed up in five easy lessons:

- **Be yourself. If you're not, people will see through it in a nanosecond.**

- **Make them feel wanted without being pushy.**

- **Offer them something irresistible without being officious; in other words, never talk down to people.**

- **Make them feel like their needs are CAB's primary concern.**

- **Give them an unqualified "win."**

These stage presentations were fun for me, and I think my relaxed approach allowed the audience to relax and therefore to be more receptive to what I was saying. It also made it easy for my salespeople to schedule one-on-one meetings with individual property managers after the fact, and I would generally spend the next few days sitting in on those.

Everyone was happy. Home sales were skyrocketing. Everyone was buying. Condominium complexes and gated communities were all the rage. The banks were parceling out home loans to everyone with an itch to buy, and they were creating things like interest only packages, adjustable rate mortgages, and outrageous refinance packages that were as irresponsible as they were irresistible.

In 2004, First National Bank of Arizona's assets topped the $2.7 billion mark. The company was riding the crest of the real estate boom and was working its magic in three of the hottest states in the country: Arizona, Nevada and California.

Community Association Banc was contributing in a big time way. From 2003 to 2004, CAB's deposits rose nearly 100% from $114 million to $222 million. That is a lot of loanable money, and builders and buyers were scrambling for it.

We had nearly a hundred clients onboard by this time. I added another three salespeople the following year, and we were making our presence felt in 20 states nationwide, with more to come. My salespeople were making money hand over fist, and my status in the industry was on the rise.

I have to admit it; I liked the attention. I liked the growing recognition of CAB and the undisputed reputation of my lockbox system. The recognition gave us the impetus to improve our technology, and every request I made for new equipment and new staff went unquestioned.

Success breeds success; it always has and it always will. Our reputation made it easier and easier for my salespeople to go into a property management firm and convince them of the advantages of CAB's personalized services. Interestingly, but not surprisingly, this unmitigated success also made me work harder. I always had a 24/7 mentality, but there was no mistaking the added adrenaline that a 100% growth rate produced.

I may have had more spring in my step, but I also had a keen appreciation for the good fortune I was experiencing.

———

Remember how we started our discussion in Chapter One. We talked about leadership as a verb. We said that leadership is about taking action, setting a positive example, and never getting complacent.

———

More risk, we said, may lead to more roadblocks and the potential for more failure, but it also generates an environment for increasing success. Even in the face of tremendous growth, the idea is to stay on the leading edge. Innovate. Improve your working model. Push the envelope.

I wasn't satisfied with $222 million in deposits. I wanted to see how far we could go.

Chapter 13

Leaders Think Smart and Work Smarter

Bar Room Economics

You have to know how to follow before you can assume the role of a leader. Not everyone is destined to be a leader. It's just not in the cards. It could be a matter of opportunity, or it could be a matter of ability or know how. It can also be a matter of desire; not every one wants the responsibilities.

Not everyone can be a strategist, the person with the grand vision or the person with his or her finger on the pulse of a situation. There have to be those people who put the strategy into play and make it work; the people we call tacticians. Both the strategist and the tactician are vital; hard to have one without the other.

But having a clear vision of the long- and short-term landscape, in particular within the world of finance and business, cannot be under-estimated. Where do you stand at any given moment in your organization, whether you're at the top of the heap or just working your way up? How can you make the most of it?

Here is one of my favorite stories, one that that paints a picture of this dynamic in a poignant, yet amusing way.

Suppose that every day, 10 men go out to their favorite haunt for beer and the bill for all 10 comes to $100. If they paid their bill the way we pay our taxes, it would go something like this:

- **The first four men (the poorest) would pay nothing.**

- **The fifth would pay $1.**

- **The sixth would pay $3.**

- **The seventh would pay $7.**

- **The eighth would pay $12.**

- **The ninth would pay $18.**

- **The tenth man (the richest) would pay $59.**

So, that's what these men decided to do. Every day, they shared a beer at the bar and seemed quite happy with their payment arrangement. And then one day, the owner threw them a curve.

"Since you're all such good customers," he said, "I'm going to reduce the cost of your daily consumption of beer by $20."

So from then on, the drinks for the 10 men would now cost just $80 instead of the normal $100. What a deal!

The group still wanted to pay their bill the way we pay our taxes, so the first four men were unaffected. They would still drink for free. But what about the other six men? The paying customers? How could they divide the $20 windfall so that everyone would get his "fair share?" They realized that $20 divided by six was $3.33. But if they subtracted that from everybody's share, then the fifth man and the sixth man would each end up being "paid" to drink his beer. So, the bar owner suggested that it would be fair to reduce each man's bill by roughly the same percentage, and he proceeded to work out the amounts each should pay. Here's how it went:

- **The fifth man, like the first four, now paid nothing (100% savings).**

- **The sixth now paid $2 instead of $3 (33%savings).**

- **The seventh now pay $5 instead of $7 (28%savings).**

- **The eighth now paid $9 instead of $12 (25% savings).**

- **The ninth now paid $14 instead of $18 (22% savings).**

- **The tenth now paid $49 instead of $59 (16% savings).**

Each of the six was better off than before. And the first four continued to drink for free. But once they got outside the restaurant, the men began to compare their savings.

"Hold on, I only got a dollar out of the $20," declared the sixth man. He pointed to the tenth man. "But he got $10!"

"Yeah, that's right," exclaimed the fifth man, also pointing at the tenth man. "I only saved a dollar, too. If you ask me, it's unfair that he got back ten times more than I did!"

"That's true!!" shouted the seventh man. "Why should he get $10 back when I got only two? The wealthy get all the breaks!"

"Wait a minute," yelled the first four men in unison. "We didn't get anything at all. The system exploits the poor!"

The nine men surrounded the tenth guy and proceeded to beat him up.

The next night the tenth man didn't show up for drinks, so the nine sat down and had beers without him. But when the bartender brought them the their bill, they discovered something important. They realized that they didn't have enough money among all of them for even half of the bill!

That's how it works, whether it's our tax system or the organizational chart of a corporation. The people who pay the highest taxes get the most benefit from a tax reduction. The people who have risen the highest in an organization have more responsibility, have more authority, and get paid more. And they usually take the biggest hit when things go bad.

I usually end this story by saying, "For those of you who understand, no further explanation is needed. For those of you who don't, no explanation is possible."

Smart and Smarter

Back in Chapter 5, we talked about Stephen Covey's Circle of Concern and Circle of Influence. The higher up you go on the organizational chart, the greater your potential "circle of concern" can be. There are more people, issues, events, and situations that may very well factor into your world and cause you concern. But the thing that does NOT change is the fact that there will always remain only a finite number of people, issues, events, and situations that you can truly influence or control by your actions and your decisions. Those are the things you must give your attention to.

This is why I always contend that the most effective leaders think smart and work smarter. It's not enough to keep your head above water, even in tough times.

An effective leader finds new ways to succeed, new strategies to employ, and new ways of motivating his or her team. An effective leader knows that risk is a road worth traveling, but he or she also knows that thinking smarter and working harder helps mitigate the risk, and may even turn the risk into a positive.

Taking Care of Business

CAB was its own entity within the First National Bank Holding Company, which was the name given to the parent company of First National Bank of Arizona, First National Bank of Nevada, and Heritage Bank, all banks owned by Ray Lamb. The company pursued four key businesses: commercial lending, construction lending, small business loans, and mortgages.

In 2005, the company was on fire. Including the company's retail division, it now employed more than 2,000 people. Assets during that year exceeded the $3 billion mark. Community Association Banc, which now had a sales staff nationwide of 10 people, brought in $556 million in deposits by the end of the year. We now had nearly 300 customers in the form of property management companies who were now banking with us. Ray's holding company owned three banks, so we were spreading the money through the system to maximize FDIC insurance parameters. The FDIC insurance was good up to $100,000. So if, hypothetically, a homeowner's association had $250,000 in deposits, my division managers might deposit $100,000 in First National Bank of Arizona, a like amount in First National Bank of Nevada, and the balance in Heritage Bank.

This is just one example of the many policies and procedures we implemented as CAB grew.

People were still building, and people were still buying. Which meant, in this environment, that banks were still lending at a furious rate.

Outside of FNB's footprint of Nevada and Arizona, CAB now had offices or a full time presence in Boston, Charlotte, Chicago and Seattle, to go with our original five markets (Houston, Dallas, Denver, Minneapolis, and Washington DC).

I was traveling constantly. By this time, I was more the guru of the operation, the guy who regularly came in and made presentations to packed houses filled with prospective homeowners associations and property management groups. I loved the model we had created. Even though I was no longer doing the same amount of hands-on sales I once had been, I was finding a niche that I thoroughly enjoyed and which was proving highly successful for my salespeople. I was the CAB presence that the customer could point to; the guy who made working with an Arizona-based bank desirable. My salespeople were the customers' immediate points of contact; they were the people who greased the customer service wheels, kept the candy jars filled in their offices, and made the rounds on a regular basis. They were the people who worked the trenches just as I had done when the division was first getting off the ground.

We had a regular Monday morning conference call that the entire team participated in. We always kept it positive. If there was new business to discuss, we always took care of that first thing. Then we opened it up to everyone: Share a story, an anecdote, a laugh. The idea was to create a community among a group of salespeople who were scattered all over the country. Most of them worked out of home offices and were more or less out there on their own. They needed to know that wasn't the case. We were a team. I had their backs. The Monday morning call was a way for me to show my support for them on the one hand, but it was also a way for them to support each other on the other hand: positive team building.

These were good times. Everyone was making exceptional money.

But exceptional money also creates another dilemma for the leader of an organization. How do you avoid complacency? How do you challenge your people to extend themselves, to push themselves a little harder, to go that extra mile? You do it by setting the best example possible through your own actions. You do it by getting down in the trenches with them and showing them how much you appreciate their efforts. You do it by a pat on the back, a well-timed compliment, or an unexpected reward. You do it by reinforcing goals and reinventing strategies.

———

I believe in loyalty. I believe that loyalty is a two-way street; you can't expect it if you don't show it. But loyalty is not something that just magically happens.

———

Loyalty is a by-product of strong relationships, and nothing motivates people like a committed investment in a mutually gratifying relationship. The workplace is no different than any other part of your life when it comes to this. You have to do it with your spouse, your friends, and co-workers.

As it had always been throughout my working life, I knew that building strong, loyal relationships with my salespeople, whether they were in Denver, Colorado or Charlotte, North Carolina, was the key in motivating them above and beyond the money they were making.

The very same rule applies to our customers. Big or small, every customer deserves the royal treatment. If for some reason you can't provide it, then don't solicit their business.

———

The highest compliment a customer can pay me is to recommend me to another prospective client. That tells me I've been successful as a businessman, a partner, and a human being.

———

I was attending an industry conference recently when a property manager I'd signed up nearly four years before came up to me and said hello. When we first met, he was only working with three or four homeowners associations at the time, and he'd been turned down by any number of banks because he "just wasn't big enough." Well, he was big enough for us, and I could see that he had what it took to be successful. We signed him up. Now, four years later, he had grown to 50 or 60 homeowner groups and was doing great.

He pulled me aside at the conference and said, "Craig, I've got a story I just have to tell you. Every week the rep from the big bank downtown comes into my office, and every week he asks me when I'm going to start banking with him. This is the same guy who turned me down when I was getting started four years ago. I remember him saying back then, 'Oh, you're too small. We can't do business with you.' Now, every time he comes in asking for my business, I tell him, 'Do you really think I'm going to move from CAB? Where were you when I needed your help four years ago?'"

He looked at me and said, "You were there for me, Craig, and I'll always appreciate that."

That's loyalty. Loyalty is earned. It's a long-term commitment. You can't put a price tag on loyalty. It's invaluable. Unfortunately, too many people don't see it. They think in the short term. And while the short term is important, it's in the longterm where success truly lies.

In-N-Out Burger

If you're not from the west coast, you may never have heard of In-N-Out Burger. In-N-Out was founded in 1948 and became California's first drive-through hamburger stand. I've eaten my fair share of In-N-Out burgers – best burger in the world – and would recommend them in a heartbeat, especially if you order it "Animal Style."

In the beginning, the founders sold 7-Up from their drink fountain. Try to find a drive-through that serves 7-Up these days. It's either Pepsi or Coke, Coke or Pepsi. Sure, In-N-Out serves Coke too, and root beer. But every time Coke offers to put Sprite into their restaurants for free, the owners say, "No way. 7-Up was there when we started. They gave us machines when no one else would. 7-Up is our brand, and we're not giving them up for anything, even free Sprite."

Now that's loyalty. That's building a relationship, nurturing it, and sticking with it through thick and thin. We said it before, but it bears repeating: strong relationships are at the heart of most success stories.

The Goose That Laid the Golden Egg

We've all heard this ancient fable attributed to the storyteller Aesop. I have adopted it as a regular aside whenever I talk about leadership.

Ancient it may be, but its message could hardly be more relevant to our times.

As the story goes, a man and his wife have the good fortune of owning a beautiful silver goose that just happens to lay one golden egg each and every day. Lucky though the couple was, they eventually got it in their heads that they were not getting rich fast enough. Just imagine, if this amazing goose can lay a golden egg every day, they thought, then it must be made of gold on the inside. So they decided to kill it. That way, they could have all the gold all at once. Unfortunately, though not surprisingly, they found upon cutting the poor bird open that it was just like any other goose on the inside. No gold, no instant wealth, no satisfying their greed. Instead, what they got was the instant end to their good fortune.

Today, "killing the golden goose" has become a metaphor for any short-sighted action that may bring an immediate reward, but ultimately proves disastrous. We've all seen it happen.

There are also a couple of other worthwhile lessons here:

- **Recognize that greed is a killer, pure and simple; it has a way of trumping just about anything that is truly good.**

- **Even in the pursuit of the most ambitious goals, be satisfied with what you have at any given moment.**

- **In any good business deal, all parties need to be winners.**

- **Think before you act.**

We had a good thing going with CAB. We had created something that worked, a business model that was advantageous and profitable for all the parties concerned. The property management groups were saving an extraordinary amount of time and money using our lock-box system to process, deposit, and record thousands upon thousands of checks every day. The homeowners associations were profiting from a steady stream of interest income on the money that they had deposited in our banks. And our banks were generating exceptional profits on the loans they were able to make from deposits CAB was bringing in every month.

By the end of 2006, that number had soared to an extraordinary $1.15 billion in deposits.

Effectiveness

I talk about this subject a lot when I'm speaking to industry groups around the country.

––––––

I define effectiveness this way: Effectiveness is getting superb results today – what I call "production" – in a way that allows us to get those results over and over again – what I call "production capital."

––––––

"Production" is getting the job done. "Production capital" is taking care of the engine. It makes sense, doesn't it?

So, for example, if you have a goose that produces a golden egg every day – production – you want to provide that goose with the best grain, comfortable and protected shelter, and lots of love – production capital.

If you want to enjoy a healthy body and an active lifestyle – production – then make a point of maintaining a healthy diet and committing yourself to regular exercise – production capital.

If, as a leader, you are focusing on developing the various talents of your staff to their fullest, and if your goal is to see them maximizing those talents in the workplace – production – then don't kill them by pushing them to their limits every day – production capital. In other words, encourage them to spend quality time with their families. Encourage them to exercise on a regular basis. Praise their efforts in front of their peers. Reward their efforts with something special like a getaway to Las Vegas, a monthly dinner at the restaurant of their choice, or a golf outing with their significant other. You get the picture.

———

Treat everyone in life – personal or professional – like human beings with hopes and dreams and simple desires, and they will go that extra mile for you.

———

Here's a more personal story, and one that is close to my heart, probably because I realized a long time ago how important are the people who work for you.

This happened back in 1985. I still owned my property management company. By then, we had grown by leaps and bounds and had 25 people working in the office. It was the Christmas season, and I always tried to do something special for my staff during the holidays. But what was I going to do for them this Christmas? The usual Christmas party just wasn't going to make it. I wanted something they would remember beyond a glass of spiked eggnog.

So two days before Christmas, we had our mandatory midday office meeting. Everyone crowded into our conference room, wondering what the heck was going on. I pointed to five of my staff and said, "You're all driving. Everyone pile into their cars and follow me."

Ten minutes later, our mini caravan arrived at the local mall, and everyone followed me inside to the food court. I jumped up on one of the tables and gathered everyone around. Quite a sight! One by one, I passed out 25 sealed envelopes with each of their names written across the front.

"Inside is $250," I told them. "You have four hours to spend it. But hereare the rules. You have to spend it on yourselves. You can't spend it on your kids, on your spouse, or on groceries. You can't buy socks for your daughter or a tie for your husband. You can't pay the electric bill. You have to spend it on yourself. Every penny of it. And you have to buy something special. This is $250 to buy that something you've always wanted. In four hours, you have to come back here with your receipts and show me what you bought and give me back any change from the $250. Have fun!"

I had high hopes for the idea, but never would have believed how successful the experience turned out to be. My office clerk, JT, a single mom, came back with a bottle of $250 perfume and tears in her eyes. She hugged me and said, "I've wanted this perfume my whole life and would never in a million years buy it for myself. I'll treasure it."

One of our maintenance people, a guy who loved to cook, came back with a new set of pots and pans, beaming from ear to ear. One of our accountants splurged on a new sport coat. One of our managers treated herself to a complete gardening set. On and on, one happy shopper after another came back with that same look. It was special for all of us, but it was particularly special for me as an employer.

———

Here was a chance to pat someone on the back in a way they would remember for a long time, a simple way of saying thank you.

———

Here was a simple way of making a group of hard workers feel completely appreciated. Or, as we said earlier, "taking care of the engine" so the results of their efforts don't diminish over time.

Production and production capital are inexorably linked, and the manager who doesn't recognize this will find his staff hitting the wall at some point. And when this happens, it's not only production that suffers; morale, enthusiasm, and energy all take a hit as well.

Somebody once said, "People don't care how much you know until you show them how much you care."

That's not just some clever saying. It's the absolute truth. And any leader worth his or her salt understands that getting the best out of your people is directly related to the respect you show them.

CAB had 18 salespeople by the end of 2006, and we were active in 42 states. One part of my job was to help them get the job done: in other words, cultivating new accounts while effectively servicing existing accounts. Another part was to help them maintain the engine; in other words, reminding them that they had lives outside of work, and that those lives were what made the job important in the first place.

Thinking smart and working smarter is not a part time job for an effective leader. It applies to people, products, and strategies both up and down the chain of command. A good leader doesn't blame a failed strategy on the people higher up the ladder. And a good leader always gives credit to the people on the rungs further down the ladder when things do go well.

Thinking smart and working smarter doesn't mean all of your decisions are going to be popular. We all have to make unpopular decisions.

Thinking smart and working smarter doesn't mean you're going to be liked by everyone. It's not going to happen, and you shouldn't worry about it.

But thinking smart and working smarter does suggest that you're taking action and, as we've already determined, that is the definition of leadership.

Chapter 14

Think Before You Communicate

When Times Get Rough

We've talked about risk. We've talked about the fact that risk is an inherent part of any venture. No one can identify every pitfall that a business is going to face, no matter how optimistic the outlook.

Much like life itself, the business environment is a malleable thing. Change is the only thing you can count on without exception. Change is what makes new products and new ideas great. But change is also the thing that can throw an unexpected wrench into the machine and knock your well-planned strategy into the dead zone.

———

What you do in these times of crisis is really what defines you as a businessman or businesswoman. It's what defines your character. And it's your character, as we said earlier, that defines your destiny.

———

What kind of leader have you become? Have you satisfied our definition of effective leadership by taking action, by getting down in the trenches and making things happen, by setting the best example possible? Has your willingness to take action and lead in a proactive way fostered habits that will see you through even the most trying of times?

It's relatively easy to be a good leader when times are good and everything seems to be falling your way. But tough times bring out either the best in a person or the worst. We've all heard the cliché about how setbacks can really be turned into opportunities, but this can be a lot easier said than done.

I like the guy who said, "The only thing that overcomes hard luck is hard work." That's a statement filled with hope, and that's another thing an effective leader provides: hope. Sometimes it's the very best thing you can provide.

The Blindside

My first experience with a failing bank was back in the mid-1990s. The name of the bank is not important, but this happened while I was still charging ahead with my property management company, Huntington Property Services. In those days, the FDIC insured all deposits up to $100,000.

It was key at the time to make certain that none of my homeowners associations had more than $100,000 in any one bank, just as a precaution. No one ever expects banks to fail. However, it's a terrible misnomer that banks are somehow sacrosanct or inviolate. They're not. We've seen enough examples of that in the last two years. Banks are run by regular people who make mistakes just like any businessman or woman, and sometimes those mistakes can be catastrophic.

Unbeknownst to me, one of my account managers had deposited $200,000 from one of our customers in two different branches of the same savings and loan, thinking she had fulfilled our requirements of placing no more than $100,000 in any one bank. When the S&L in question failed, this particular homeowners association stood to lose $50,000. I was at fault. Even if it was an honest mistake on the part of my account manager – and it certainly was – I was responsible. The old adage about "the buck stops here" applied in full in this case. I broke out the company checkbook on the spot and wrote the association a $50,000 check. That was a lot of money back then. It's a lot of money today too.

It was an expensive lesson. I never again took for granted the state of the economy, or relaxed in the face of good times. Good times require the same amount of diligence as hard times; they require the same focus and the same work ethic.

―――――

The minute you begin to take for granted your good fortune might well be the very moment when you should be most prepared to deal with adversity.

―――――

I'm not suggesting for a moment that you shouldn't enjoy your successes. You should. But taking your successes for granted is not the same thing as enjoying your successes. You don't want to be blindsided. You want to be prepared, diligent, and ready when adversity strikes. And strike it will.

The Smoke Before the Fire

The late 1990s and most of the last decade in the housing industry illustrated in no uncertain terms the problems that ensue when people walk that fine line between the ethical and the non-ethical, and crash full force over the line of responsible behavior. The subprime fiasco was a disaster waiting to happen, and deep down inside everyone knew it. You don't lend money to people without the means to repay the loan, and rationalizing it by believing the government is there to help you is a serious mistake.

―――――

Banks and mortgage companies were making money hand over fist. Real estate investors were making money hand over fist. Homebuyers were convinced that they would make money hand over fist because the housing market was bulletproof.

―――――

The truth got buried in an avalanche of misinformation, mis-communications, and pie-in-the-sky nonsense. Was it malicious? Not at First National Bank. Everyone wants a piece of a good thing, and we all have the ability to convince ourselves that things won't go wrong. The housing market had been bullish for so long that common sense and good judgment often fell victim to the euphoria of the times.

Our own banks – First National Bank of Arizona, First National Bank of Nevada, and Heritage Bank – were flying as high as you could get over an eight-year period. Assets topped $4.3 billion in 2006, helped by a boom in lower-quality "Alt-A" mortgages. These are mortgages that are rated somewhere in between prime and subprime loans. But the luster was fading by year's end.

Community Association Banc (whose operations had nothing to do with the mortgage industry per se, other than the fact that the deposits we were bringing in were fodder for real estate and building loans of all kinds) continued its amazing rise. We broke the billion-dollar mark in deposits in March of 2007. The division had 18 salesmen and women working most of the United States and making small fortunes themselves. CAB, a single division of First National Holding, was itself bigger than most banks. We were one of the most profitable banking entities in the country.

But there was something in the air. I had long wondered how all of these subprime loans were getting made and where the borrowers were getting the money to make payments they had no business taking on. I also had to wonder how long this euphoric rush of endless optimism could last.

Sure enough the first warning signs appeared in early 2007, even as our division was raking in record profits. First National Holding was targeted in lawsuits brought by Lehman Brothers and several others, who claimed that the firm had sold them bad mortgages without effectively verifying income, employment status, and other relevant information from borrowers.

The smoke before the fire grew a little thicker a month later, when the downturn in mortgage lending became even more apparent. This was a definite blow, and First National was forced to announce its first layoffs ever. Over 200 people were given their walking papers; this represented nearly 10% of our work force. Our three banks still employed 2,000 people, including branches and the company's wholesale division, but it was not a good sign.

Communication 101

We've all heard the statement: Think before you speak. My parents must have said that to me a thousand times.

But whenever I have occasion to speak to groups about communication and personal relationships, I like to take that statement a little further. For me, it should read: *Think before you communicate.*

This is a chart I like to use in the course of this conversation. Take a look and be prepared to be amazed:

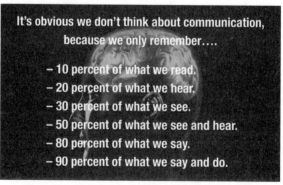

It's obvious we don't think about communication, because we only remember....

- 10 percent of what we read.
- 20 percent of what we hear.
- 30 percent of what we see.
- 50 percent of what we see and hear.
- 80 percent of what we say.
- 90 percent of what we say and do.

Source: Purdue University Department of Organizational Leadership and Supervision

The message here is that communication is a combination of many things. Speaking is only one component, and clearly way down the list when it comes to being a successful communicator. Listening is really at the heart of learning, and yet we are often so busy preparing our response or discounting what someone is saying that we miss the learning part. We often hear what we want to hear rather than truly listening. We often see what we want to see rather than what's really there.

Very often it's not the content that matters as much as it is the deliverer of the message, and his or her delivery.

Two people can attempt to communicate the very same thing, and yet one can completely miss the mark just because he fails in his delivery.

There is no better (or more fun) example of this than the age-old story of "Paul Revere and His Midnight Ride." As the story goes, on the night of April 18, 1775, a silversmith named Paul Revere left his small wooden home in Boston's North End on a borrowed horse and set out on a journey that would make him into a legend, riding as far as Lexington and Concord shouting, "The British are coming, the British are coming," calling all men to arms along the way.

We all know the story. Paul's successful ride was revered in a legendary poem by Longfellow, and his name was taken by a 60s rock group called Paul Revere and the Raiders.

What most people don't know is that Paul wasn't the only guy sent out that night to warn of the British attack. Have you ever heard of William Dawes? Most people haven't. Dawes set out that same night with the same goal as Paul Revere, but he took a different route and used a far less effective delivery. He had the same content and the same idea as Paul, but he couldn't get his message across. And the result? No one remembers the poor guy. No one wrote a poem memorializing him and nary a rock group was named after him.

The point is that choosing your method of communication, picking your words judiciously, and giving careful consideration to your timing is essential. Over the years, I even developed a list of "good words" (words to infuse into both the spoken word and the written word) and "bad words" (words to avoid whether you're talking to an employee or sending an email).

These are words that linguists recognize as having profound influence on our physical and emotional responses, and on the responses of the man, woman, or child hearing or reading the words. Here are my lists:

Good Words

ability	courage	genuine	majority	salient
abundant	courtesy	good	merit	satisfactory
achieve	definite	grateful	notable	service
active	dependable	guarantee	opportunity	simplicity
admirable	deserving	handsome	perfection	sincerity
advance	desirable	harmonious	permanent	stability
advantage	determined	helpful	perseverance	substantial
ambition	distinction	honesty	please	success
appreciate	diversity	honor	popularity	superior
approval	ease	humor	practical	supreme
aspire	economy	imagination	praiseworthy	thorough
attainment	effective	improvement	prestige	thoughtful
authoritative	efficient	industry	proficient	thrift
benefit	energy	ingenuity	progress	truth
capable	enhance	initiative	prominent	truthful
challenge	enthusiasm	integrity	propriety	useful
cheer	equality	intelligence	punctual	utility
comfort	excellence	judgment	reasonable	valuable
commendable	exceptional	justice	recognition	vigor
comprehensive	exclusive	kind	recommend	vivid
concentration	expedite	lasting	reliable	wisdom
confidence	faith	liberal	reputable	you
conscientious	fidelity	life	responsive	yours
cooperation	fitting	loyalty	responsible	

Bad Words

abandoned	deadlock	hazy	premature	tamper
abuse	decline	ignorant	pretentious	tardy
affected	desert	illiterate	problem	timid
alibi	disaster	imitation	retrench	tolerable
allege	discredit	immature	rude	unfair
apology	dispute	implicate	ruin	unfortunate
bankrupt	evict	impossible	shirk	unsuccessful
beware	exaggerate	improvident	shrink	untimely
biased	extravagant	insolvent	sketchy	verbiage
blame	failure	meager	slack	waste
calamity	fault	misfortune	smattering	weak
cheap	fear	muddle	split	worry
collapse	flagrant	negligence	squander	wrong
collusion	flat	obstinate	stagnant	
commonplace	flimsy	oversight	standstill	
complaint	fraud	plausible	straggling	
crisis	gratuitous	precipitate	stunned	
crooked	hardship	prejudiced	superficial	

On the surface, there may not appear to be anything magical or revelatory about these lists, but I would ask you to take a second look. Picture yourself in an important business meeting or discussing a critical issue with your spouse. Imagine the conversation you're having and allow a number of the "bad words" to creep into the conversation. It's not too difficult to predict the negative impact, is it? Then play the same conversations back again and commit yourself to using only words from our "good words" list. The difference is extraordinary.

If you're having difficulty with that, imagine replying to an important email, one that may have caused an emotional reaction on your part, and write two responses, one tapping into the "bad words" list and the other focusing on choices from the "good words" list. Again, you'll be amazed by the potential impact of each.

Think before you communicate. Think before you let your tongue get away from you. And think before you pound out a bunch of words on your computer that you might regret later.

Those few seconds or few minutes that you allow yourself to gather your thoughts can be the difference between effective communication and disastrous results. When emotions run deep, waiting a day is not a bad thing.

Thinking before you communicate is a skill. It takes conscious effort. And it rarely fails to be the best approach.

When Behavior Speaks Louder Than Words

Communication is more than just talking, listening, and responding. It's more than penning emails or sending memos.

Behavior speaks volumes. Body language is unmistakable. If you think you can say one thing while your behavior and body language are saying another and expect to fool anyone, you're playing with fire. Behavior can either enhance or inhibit communications, and I like to demonstrate this with two very telling lists. Take a look at these and picture yourself on both sides of these six behavioral traits and the messages they send:

Six Behaviors That Inhibit Communication

1 Judging *("You're Wrong")*

2 Superiority *("Clearly I am better than you")*

3 Certainty *("Don't confuse me with the facts. My mind's made up")*

4 Controlling *("Let me tell you how to do things right!")*

5 Manipulation *("Gotcha")*

6 Indifference *("Whatever. You're not important and neither are your ideas")*

It is easy to imagine how quickly these six behaviors can bring effective and meaningful communication to an immediate halt. More importantly, it's easy to see how quickly the intended results of a conversation or a correspondence can be compromised by them.

On the opposite side of the fence are six positive behaviors and the messages they impart. Have a look:

Six Behaviors That Enhance Communication

1. Description
The opposite of Judging. The person applying Description is seen as seeking information about ideas to more fully understand them. The person uses words and creates perceptions that don't imply others are wrong or need to change.

2. Equality
The opposite of Superiority. Communication is enhanced when you treat others with trust, respect and deference. Differences in power, authority, intelligence and creativity often exist but the effective communicator puts little importance in these differences.

3. Openness
The opposite of Certainty. The person using Openness is not closed to ideas of others and never takes sides. Rather they are seen as investigating issues and as problem solvers. They exhibit an interest in a shared approach to meeting challenges. Partnership is a strong perception here.

Six Behaviors That Enhance Communication

4. Problem-Orientation

The opposite of Controlling. When a person communicates a desire to work together to define a problem or seek a solution he/she is seen as asking questions, seeking information and having no predetermined solution.

5. Positive Intent

The opposite of Manipulation. Behavior and words that appear to be spontaneous and free of deception encourage communication. The perception of honesty and spontaneity creates less defensiveness in others.

6. Empathy

The opposite of Indifference. Empathy reflects feelings and respect for the worth of the person you are communicating with. The communicator exhibiting empathy uses words and behaviors that show they identify with the feelings and problems of the receiver, and accepts the receiver's reactions and responses at face value.

Situations don't dictate whether good or bad behavior is in order, any more than situations dictate whether good words or bad words are in order. If your intent is effective communication, then every situation calls for the good in both. Crisis situations may be more trying and call for more tact and diplomacy, but this only reinforces the need for an effective leader to understand how to make the best of every situation.

A Bad Moon Rising

I knew there was a crisis situation looming in my future.

I knew there were problems brewing in the banking and housing industries before the crisis of 2007 really hit full force. Subprime loans had negative consequences written all over them. All it would take was a moderate downturn in housing prices and, with a recession clearly looming in the future of the U.S. economy, it didn't take much to tip the scales. Housing prices had celebrated an extraordinary boom cycle, which began in 1997 and rose an astounding 83% until the wheels came off in July of 2006 and the market began to freefall.

Now what? No more appreciation. No more windfall profits. No more adjustable rate mortgages or subprime loans on houses "guaranteed" to be worth far more than they were when they were purchased. The prosperity bubble had clearly burst, and the results were predictable.

You know the rest of the story. We're living it even today.

But looking out at the crisis from an insider's perspective, the story took its own unique, if equally devastating turn. First National Holdings and its three banks, where all of Community Association Banc's deposits were being held, were under extraordinary pressure from failing loans and a sudden paralysis within the mortgage industry as a whole.

In August of 2007, First National announced 541 more layoffs and plans to close its wholesale-mortgage operation. This was ominous news.

That same month, CAB dropped $30 million in deposits. The following month we battled back and actually added $32 million in deposits, showing total deposits of $1.1 billion. But I had to wonder what the next months would bring as our parent company began to tally up losses.

Our salespeople were still out there selling our lockbox system, which remained the strongest and most technically sound by far in the industry. Were our profits enough to save the mother ship? I didn't honestly think so. But I also felt that the strength of CAB's position in the industry would lessen the blow in the long run.

The first quarter of 2008, First National reported a $140 million loss; sure all banks were struggling by this time, but the shortfall First National suffered was several times larger than the red ink tallied up by all the other troubled banks in Arizona combined. Even though CAB's deposits had risen to a record high $1.3 billion, we were showing nearly $300 million over the FDIC insurance rate. If the bank had gone down that day, our customers would have lost $300 million, and I could not allow that to happen.

———

I would later tell people that had that happened, I would have been checking the underside of my car with a mirror, because seeing a well-placed stick of dynamite down there would not have surprised me in the least. It was that serious.

———

Had such a thing happened, the chain reaction would have been unprecedented. The homeowners associations would have sued the management companies, and the management companies would have come after us. And who could have blamed them? Even though CAB had nothing to do with the operational side of First National's banking group, I felt responsible. These were our customers. These were people who had put their trust in us.

We very quietly began encouraging people to redistribute their deposits, being very careful not to create a panic. This was a poignant, telling example of the "think before you communicate" principle, walking a fine line between serving our clients and causing them harm, balancing good words and bad words, as it were. Our goal was to protect them without tipping the precarious scale upon which the bank was operating. It became obvious our efforts to see these uninsured deposits redistributed weren't happening fast enough.

And then, an opportunity to positively affect the situation presented itself, and I knew I had to take it. As the crisis surrounding the bank worsened, the regulators from the FDIC paid a visit to my office. Their intent was to interview me regarding the Community Association Banc's position within the First National Holding hierarchy, and I used the interview to state my case in no uncertain terms.

I needed one example that even the Feds could understand. I needed an example that would clearly illustrate to them what might happen if they didn't step in and insure all of our funds immediately. I chose the Watergate, the hotel and luxury apartment complex made famous by the 1972 burglary perpetrated by President Nixon's re-election committee.

One of the management companies who banked with us managed the Watergate. It just so happened that Elizabeth Dole, former Secretary of Transportation and wife of U.S. Senator Bob Dole, was on the Watergate's board of directors. Or at least she had been at some point; I didn't care. I just needed a point of leverage. And it just so happened that the Watergate had $1.2 million in deposits in our bank, about $900,000 of which was uninsured.

And that's what I told my FDIC interviewers. I said, "Here's the thing. If you don't insure all of the funds in our bank, Elizabeth Dole and her board of directors are going to lose $900,000. Do you know what that means? Can you imagine the repercussions that will have across the country?"

I could see it on their faces at that very moment. A light bulb went on. I could almost hear them saying, "Oh, so this isn't just an Arizona and Nevada problem. These guys are nationwide."

"We're in 42 states, guys," I said. "This problem is going to explode, and we're going to have homeowners associations from California to Washington DC filing lawsuits. It's going to get really ugly if you don't jump in and make sure every deposit in our bank is insured down to the last cent."

That did it. I suddenly had an ally. It didn't save the bank, but it relieved me of the need to examine the underside of my car with a mirror every day.

———

Communication that is well thought out is a key element in moving any situation in a positive direction, but it is an absolute must in a crisis situation. How you present your case can mean the difference between averting disaster and going down in flames.

———

Turn Out the Lights

Most of us knew the bank was going to fail because the capital-to-asset ratio had dropped dramatically. The bank no longer had the capital to cover its losses, and the federal regulators had been watching the situation like hawks for many months.

The FDIC has a rating system that goes by the inauspicious acronym C.A.M.E.L. The system tracks five component areas: Capital adequacy, Asset quality, Management, Earnings, and Liquidity. They use a simple 1 to 5 rating system, 1 being the highest possible score. It was pretty well known in the industry that First National's rating had been sky high for years, probably a 2, though I can't say that for certain. From 2001 through 2004, the regulators thought we were the greatest banking operation on the planet. Come 2007, it was pretty well known in the industry that we'd taken a serious fall in every category.

If, by some chance, there was a run on the bank and people started demanding their money, there wasn't enough in the vaults to cover it, á la 1929.

By June of 2008, Ray Lamb and his team were doing everything in their power to salvage the situation. Ray replaced his longtime CEO and President. Amid a swirl of rumors regarding the firm's troubles, First National Bank of Arizona merged into First National Bank of Nevada in a bid to improve the capital position of the resulting entity. It wasn't enough.

On the morning of Friday, July 25, an email was sent out to all the pertinent executives of the bank – including me – that something was in the wind. A conference call was scheduled. The call was short and sweet. Our CFO had been informed that the bank was closing. In his words, "The Feds are taking over. Cooperate with them in every way you can."

———

Those are not the words any banker wants to hear, especially after the entity that we had built with CAB was so successful.
At 4:30 in the afternoon, the Feds walked into every First National Holding branch from Las Vegas to Phoenix and announced, "We're taking over."

———

To Ray Lamb, my longtime friend and a truly honorable banker, they said, "You no longer own this bank." Those may not have been their exact words, but the meaning was unmistakable.

It was an extraordinary, heart wrenching experience. The bank I had been promoting as innovative, progressive, and pioneering was out of business. All of a sudden, the government was completely in control. From that moment on, the entities known as First National Bank of Arizona and the First National Bank of Nevada no longer existed. The Federal authorities even insisted that every piece of letterhead, every pen, every business card, every notepad, everything with the First National name on it be destroyed. This is not an exaggeration.

I was certainly not happy that this mandate also included the letterhead, pens, and business cards of CAB, and I made my point with the Feds. I pointed to stacks of cards and stationery with the Community Association Banc logo imprinted on them, and argued that the division was a stand-alone entity that would continue to operate even under government supervision. They finally saw the logic behind this and backed off. CAB's materials would remain intact, even while our association with the bank was being erased.

It was a small victory and had no effect on the instantaneous demise of a bank that 24 hours before had been serving thousands of customers.

No advance notice of the takeover was given to the public. It never is when a financial institution is closed. The hope, of course, is that no one's life will be adversely affected if everything falls into place the way the government claims it will.

A Cease and Desist Order was issued. A Memorandum of Understanding was disseminated. And the FDIC agreed to sell the bank's assets.

My life was about to change in a very big way.

The good news was that a new world awaited me.

Chapter 15

The Truth About Risk

The Imperfect Road

One of the hardest things on earth to do is ignore the opinions of others, and act on what you firmly believe is in your best interest and in the best interest of those who are most important to you. To do that, you have to believe without equivocation in the pursuit you've embarked upon and you have to believe wholeheartedly in whatever it is you're trying to create.

You don't need approval for your actions, not if you believe in them. We've been talking about that throughout this book.

We also have been talking about risk and about the fact that risk is a road worth traveling. "Nothing ventured, nothing gained," may have a quaint ring to it, but there are really no truer words when it comes to pursuing your dreams. We succeed because we're willing to fail. It's as simple as that. We all have to deal with the fear of failure.

—————

Like we have been saying, failure and success are part of the same package. No one succeeds 100% of the time.

—————

I had taken a calculated risk when I sold my property management company in California and uprooted my family for an unproven venture in Las Vegas.

Ray Lamb had taken a risk when he brought me on board and allowed me to institute my lockbox system in his then-fledgling bank.

Now I was about to embark on another venture, and it would surely be filled with risk and reward, ups and downs, excitement and anxiety.

I was leaving a situation that had been filled with promise and uncertainly when I began, and I planned on finding an opportunity with equal promise. Yes, the uncertainty would be there as well. I welcomed it. Moving from certainty to uncertainty puts you on a path of growth and change.

We all seek transformation. Age has nothing to do with it; neither does our station in life at any time.

The demise of First National Bank of Arizona was terribly sad, but now I had a chance to add to the legacy I had built in pushing Community Association Banc to the top of the HOA banking world. I might not reach that particular summit again, but having a new mountain to summit reminded me how much I enjoyed the journey.

Time to Move On

When is it time to move on?

This is a huge dilemma for anyone who has put himself or herself on the line and been willing to risk falling flat. It is a huge dilemma for anyone who has dared to follow a dream. I had pulled up stakes in my late 40s, sold an established business, and decided to become a banker. My family had taken a huge leap of faith, given up the security of life in southern California, and followed me to the desert.

The result was an extraordinarily successful new venture, a string of positives, and few regrets. We had given birth to a new wave in HOA banking, had taken the concepts of the lockbox and elevated them to new levels of operation and profitability, and built a team that worked like a well-oiled machine. The last eight years had been fun. I had cultivated some of the most meaningful relationships of my life.

With the passing of the torch, I fully intended to rekindle the fun and cultivate an entire circle of new and meaningful relationships.

Leadership, as we discussed on page one, is a verb. We defined it as taking action. That was exactly what I intended to do.

Focus on What Matters

I have two rules:

- **Rule One: Don't sweat the small stuff.**
- **Rule Two: It's all small stuff.**

These rules apply to everyday life in general and to the business world in particular. Remember the personal mission statements that we discussed earlier? This is the statement that spells out what you're trying to achieve as a human being. Hopefully, you took a moment to create one for yourself. My own mission statement talks about being the best father and husband I can be, about performing random acts of kindness, about creating balance in work, play, and community, and about inspiring the people I interact with.

Whatever yours says, I think we can agree that life is clearly meant to be enjoyed. Clearly, doing the right thing is important to most of us. So is making a positive impact on the people we come in contact with during our day.

———

I use my two rules to remind myself that there are things we actually have some control over. We can focus on these kinds of things and, for the most part, be in charge of our own destiny.

———

All the rest – the small stuff – is out of our control anyway, so the less energy we give to it, the better off we are.

What Matters Most

For me, it's simple. What matters most is the honor and integrity we bring to our lives. This is not the small stuff that I referred to earlier.

This is the fabric of our existence. These are the values and principles that dictate how we're going to live our lives.

Values, as a matter of definition, are those things that really matter to us. Values are the ideas and beliefs we hold as special. We all have our list, even though I think we often forget to put words to them. For my part, I happen to value friendship and family. I value my freedom to express my opinions. I value commitment and enterprise. You get the idea.

Principles, as a matter of definition, are a man's or woman's guiding light. Principles are the absolutes that we choose to live by. I believe in kindness first. I believe in trying to find the best in everyone. I believe in giving my best. Once again, you get the idea.

Was there risk involved in seeking a new direction in my career? Certainly. But I'm a gambler. In my world, risk is a road worth traveling. I believe that if you have the leadership, the passion, and the innovation, success will follow.

Will you face problems? Will you make wrong turns? Will you fall flat on your face sometimes? Absolutely. You can't jump off the bridge into the new and unexplored without encountering problems, no matter how successful you've been in your previous ventures.

I needed a new roadmap. So I started with an old roadmap, the very one we drew up earlier:

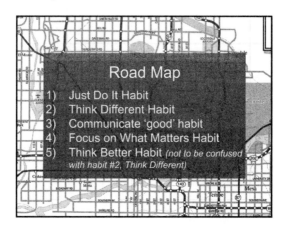

Road Map

1) Just Do It Habit
2) Think Different Habit
3) Communicate 'good' habit
4) Focus on What Matters Habit
5) Think Better Habit (not to be confused with habit #2, Think Different)

What Did We Say?

We said that the *Just Do It Habit* implies a willingness to identify your dreams – big, small, or otherwise – and to commit yourself to chasing them, even if it does lead to some rejection, disappointment, or failure.

We said that *Thinking Different* is a state of mind that looks for challenges and opportunities and isn't afraid of a little risk.

We said that *Good Communication* begins when we recognize that all effective communication is a two-way street: we send, and we receive.

We said that the *Focus on What Matters Habit* is about giving our attention to those issues that we can control and influence, not those that weigh heavy on our minds but are beyond our control.

We said that *Thinking Better* meant thinking out of the box and finding that one thing that separates you from the competition.

I had my roadmap. I felt confident I could navigate it. And that's one of the best feelings you can have.

The Road Worth Traveling

The road we're talking about, of course, is risk, and it is definitely one worth traveling down. More than that, traveling down that road is a part of leadership. Taking action, as we defined leadership, carries with it an inherent element of risk. Creating experience, which is at the leading edge of your world view, is about pushing the envelope and stepping out of your comfort zone, but mostly it's about stepping up to the plate and going for broke.

Is failure an option? Sure it is. But failure is just a bump in the road we call risk-taking.

You may want to reinvent the wheel by changing careers, or you may simply want to nudge your life in a different direction. You may have the desire to build your own business from the ground floor up, or you might be positioning yourself for a promotion to middle management. You may want to take up a whole new "lifestyle" or just shed a few pounds.

The future is unlimited. The choices we make will dictate the direction of our lives, both personally and professionally. That's an empowering thought. Are there risks involved with making choices? Of course there are. But even choosing to do nothing comes with risks.

This is life we're talking about. We all have a responsibility to make the most of it. We don't want to settle for mediocrity, and we don't want to settle for the status quo. Most of the time, we make our own opportunities, and most of the time they involve hard work, ingenuity and, yes, risk.

But I say risk is a road worth traveling. That's where the rewards are. Why not take it!

About the Author

After the FDIC took over First National Bank of Arizona and Community Association Banc it was sold to a large National Institution that did not share Craig's passion for entrepreneur spirit. Several members of his team joined him to start a new HOA division for Western Alliance Bancorp where he serves as President of Alliance Association Financial Services, a division of the bank that serves Community Associations and Management Companies throughout the United States.

Western Alliance Bancorp owns three banks, Bank of Nevada, Torrey Pines Bank (in California) and Western Alliance Bank (in Arizona).

Craig is also a well-respected and distinguished industry and motivational speaker. He has been presenting managerial, leadership and motivational presentations for the past 20 years and has developed a comprehensive collection of presentations on a wide range of subjects. Craig has spoken at CAI conferences, management companies, executive retreats and strategic meetings in over 15 states.

Craig now resides in Las Vegas Nevada with his wife Deborah.